GLORY BE, I'M ON MY KNEES

PAMELA SWEEDEN

GLORY BE, I'M ON MY KNEES

By

Pamela Sweeden

This Book is lovingly and prayerfully dedicated

To God

Who inspired me to write this book

And Who I pray will receive all the Honor and Glory.

ACKNOWLEDGEMENTS

I want to say a special thank you to many people who prayed for me and helped me along the way while writing this book.

A huge thank you goes to my editor, Helen Turner, who tirelessly worked with me, prayed with me and supported me while writing this book. I could have never done this without you, Helen!

A special thank you goes to Carroll Roberson who gave me good sound advice when I started writing this book, and to Joann Leighton who introduced the two of us.

A special thank you goes to Tom Fenix who so graciously helped draw the illustrations for this book.

And to my family members, my uncle Conley Boothe, my Aunt Jean Cunningham, my brother Dan Boothe, my sister-in-law Vickie Foster, my two sisters and brothers-in-law Ralph and Jeanette Johnson, Donald and Dorothy Holmes and to my step-grand daughter, Kelli Sweeden, and niece Judy

Juola, a big thank you for your love, support and encouragement.

Special thanks go to my best friend, Arnold Sanford, who has always supported and believed in me and prayed for me daily.

Thanks to the many good friends who have been there for me, prayed, helped and encouraged me during this time: Pastor J.D.Courtney, Pastor Sue Howe, Johnnie Minor, Nancy McLane, Tammy King, Aline Davis, Paula Martin, Tim Colclasure, Scott Smith, Brenda Edge, Lois Holcombe, Helen Tankersley, Durinda Gammill, Cynda Bellamy and Jim and Brenda Caldwell. Also, thank you to a host of many other good friends for your support.

To Toby and Sandi, my two Chihuahuas, who sat by my side patiently and sometimes not so patiently, waiting for me so I could show them some attention.

Contents

INTRODUCTION

Prayer is the key to everything in life. As we go through life's journey, we want to know there is a God in Heaven waiting to hear from us and to answer our prayers. Why is prayer such hard work, and why do we sometimes feel we are talking to the ceiling? When we have difficulties in life, where do our answers come from? All our answers come from God. He is our power source, waiting for us to call on Him.

Sin is a major reason why we don't receive answers to our prayers. If we feel our prayers are not going above the ceiling, more than likely we have unconfessed sin in our life or we are not living a Godly life. We may struggle with guilt, fear, unforgiveness, or a number of other things that would keep our prayers from being answered. We need to ask God to point out any unconfessed sin that could be obstructing our prayer life or point out areas in which we are not living God's will. We should confess our sin and ask God to help us overcome any obstacles of sin in the future.

When we have our heart right before God, God will often say yes to our prayers and will answer right away. Sometimes, He will say no to our prayers - that is not His best for us at this time. And sometimes, He just says wait, so He can give us His best or to change us in some way. Or He may want to modify our prayers to get more in line with His thoughts. Sometimes a delay in our prayer life is God's way of developing character in us, or He is testing our faith. Waiting for God to answer proves we have faith that He will answer. If the answer is no or wait a while, it could be He is waiting for us to get our heart right or to bring growth or maturity in a particular area. God will say no to our prayers if we come to Him pridefully or if we have ignored His word. (Proverbs 28:9)

We should pray and ask God to answer according to His will, not ours. We should ask ourselves if what we request would bring glory to God. We should ask if our prayers would benefit others or if they are selfish. We should ask if our request would be one Jesus would make. Would our request hinder us from growing spiritually? God is waiting for a chance to work through us and in us, if we will allow it.

When we don't know how to pray or what to pray for, the Holy Spirit intercedes on our behalf. Let us go to God humbly, as a sinner seeking after a Sovereign God. He wants His people to come to Him with a humble heart. Prayer is a privilege from God, and He has commanded us to pray.

We need to come to God with our petitions, lay them at His feet and leave them there. He wants us to come to Him with brokenness, expecting answers.

He wants to hear the fervent cries of His people. He expects us to be persistent, expecting answers. He wants us to continue to pray until we receive an answer. We need to become positive with our prayers, having no doubt that God will answer.

Prayer is the highest form of faith, and should be used frequently with expectancy. There is nothing too hard for God to do.

As we take this journey with Moses and the Israelites, let's see how much God loved His people and longed for a relationship with them. He wants a relationship with us today as much as He wanted a relationship with Israel.

May we learn through their mistakes how to pursue God, how to expect answers to our prayers, and how to never give up until we receive answers.

LOVE DIVINE

Holy Presence, Love Divine
Blessed assurance, the Lord is mine
Grace to all; love abounds
Merciful goodness, where joy resounds
Pilgrims and Saints, with boldness and power
Solemnly we pray, forgetting the hour
Believing our hearts are heard from above
Knowing He will answer, and surely with love
Yearning to hear from His loved ones so dear
Longing to hear our sweet voices so near
Love us He does; answer He will
If we refuse to allow our hearts to grow still

1

WHAT IS PRAYER?

"I AM" Exodus 3:14

We were created for a relationship, and God wants to have a relationship with each one of us. He longs to hear our voice and wants to tell us things we do not know.

Prayer is communication or conversation with God. There is no other way to commune with Him except through prayer.

"And whatever things you ask in prayer, believing, you will receive." Matthew 21:22

God will answer the prayers of His children. Sometimes He will say yes, sometimes no, sometimes wait. But He will answer in His time. His timing is not always our timing, but His timing is the right time. Sometimes it is difficult to wait, but it is to our advantage to wait on God because He sees the whole picture and knows things we do not know. Included below is the model prayer that was given to the disciples by God's Son (Jesus) in their request, "God teach us to pray."

"Our Father which art in heaven, Hallowed be Your name. Your kingdom come. Your will be done On earth, as it is in heaven. Give us this day our daily bread. And forgive us our debts, as we forgive our debtors. And do not lead us into temptation, but deliver us from the evil one: For Yours is the kingdom, and the power, and the glory, forever." Amen! Matthew 6:9-13

Let me explain what I mean in this prayer:

"Our Father which art in heaven, Hallowed (honored) be Your name."

This is praise! We should praise and honor God. He is worthy to be praised! There are several ways to praise Him. We can praise Him by telling the good news of Him, by singing of Him, by giving financially, by being baptized as a new believer, and by taking Holy Communion. It is easy to see how we praise God through telling others about him or singing about Him. How can we praise Him by giving financially or by being baptized or taking communion? When we give financially, God blesses our efforts and gives back to us more than we gave. God delights in a cheerful giver. God is a giving God and sees our heart and knows if we give willingly or begrudgingly. By being baptized, we are saying that we believe Jesus died on the cross and arose again after three days. When taking Communion, the wine or grape juice signifies the blood Jesus shed on the cross of Calvary. The wafer or unleavened bread signifies the broken body of Christ. So by acknowledging God through our actions, we praise Him.

When we worship and praise Him, it enhances our appreciation of who He is in our life. Therefore, our love grows more for Him. Worship expands our vision. When we don't worship, our vision shrinks. When we worship, we energize and refresh our spirit. Worship prepares us for the day, giving us a better attitude, giving us strength and preparing us for the day's events.

"Your kingdom come. Your will be done on earth, as it is in heaven."

When we say, "Your Kingdom come," we are saying, "God, you are my King! You are Lord of my life."

"Your will be done."

We are saying, "Your will, Lord, not mine!" We are submitting our life to God. When we submit our life to God and He takes control, He will do things we never thought possible.

"On earth as it is in heaven."

The angels in Heaven do God's will immediately, obeying God unconditionally, willingly and joyfully. When God speaks, we should be as obedient as the angels.

"Give us this day our daily bread."

God is willing to provide for our daily needs. He wants to provide over and abundantly more than we could ever imagine. He is willing to provide not only for our physical needs, but our emotional and mental needs as well.

"Forgive us our debts (sins) as we forgive our debtors."

God has asked us to forgive others as He has forgiven us.

" For if you forgive men their trespasses, your heavenly Father will also forgive you. But if you do not forgive men their trespasses, neither will your Father forgive your trespasses." Matthew 6:14-15

Unforgiveness and bitterness can destroy a person mentally, physically and spiritually. It is detrimental to our health not to forgive. I cannot stress enough the importance of getting rid of all unforgiveness and bitterness. Allowing bitterness and hatred to remain will cause inner turmoil and physical problems.

God sent His Son (Jesus) to pay a debt we could not pay for our sins. Jesus paid it all! He died on the cross to set us free from all our sins. We should forgive others as God has forgiven us. In order to forgive, we need to come to God and ask Him to help us to forgive, if we feel that our feelings are not in line with God's requirements. Forgiving others is a requirement from God, not a choice, regardless of whether we feel forgiving.

God is a Holy God and cannot look at sin. If we are willing to ask forgiveness for our sins, He is willing to forgive us. No sin is too great for God to forgive.

"Do not Lead us into temptation, but deliver us from the evil one."

God allows us to go through trials, hoping we will turn to Him for help. Our flesh is weak, and we all struggle with temptations. But if we will seek

God, He will help us overcome our temptations and weaknesses.

Satan is always ready to attack us in our weakest moments. But God is ready to deliver us from our trials and temptations, if only we would ask.

"For Yours is the kingdom, and the power, and the glory, forever."

Thank God for all His blessings. God is all-powerful, all-knowing, and deserves all the glory.

Amen!

So be it! When saying Amen, we are in agreement with God.

The Lord's Prayer is for our sanctification (being set apart for God). It is a matter of growth, and it takes a lifetime to make us holy. We can be sanctified through God's word, and every truth leads to holiness.

Therefore, as we come to God in prayer, we start out with praise and worship for Him. That really gets His attention! We ask for His will to be done in our lives and watch God change our world, step by step, little by little. We ask God for daily provisions and for help throughout the day. Also, we ask forgiveness for our sins daily, or as often as we are made aware of them. We ask God to help us avoid temptations and to deliver us from the evil one (Satan).

God has asked us to go into our secret place and pray to Him. A secret place could be a favorite chair, at the dining table, in the bed, out in a garden or park, wherever we can go and have privacy with God.

"But you, when you pray, go into your room, and when you have shut your door, pray to your Father who is in the secret place; and your Father who sees in secret will reward you openly." Matthew 6:6

When we go to our secret place, we go to God as if He were our best Friend, because He is. He wants to help us through life's difficult situations. He is there to be our Guide each and every day. He wants to protect us and shield us from Satan.

If we get into trouble throughout the day, we can go to God with our prayers, asking for help with whatever problem we may have at the time. He is always there ready to help us in our time of need.

As we start our day, we need to: "Put on the whole armor of God that you may be able to stand against the wiles of the devil." Ephesians 6:11

"For we do not wrestle against flesh and blood, but against principalities, against powers, against the rulers of the darkness of this age, against spiritual host of wickedness in the heavenly places." Ephesians 6:12

The armor of God is: The Belt of Truth, the Breastplate of Righteousness, the Sandals of Peace, the Sword of the Spirit, the Helmet of Salvation, and the Shield of Faith. (Ephesians 6:14-17)

The Belt of Truth – is girded around your waist. It helps us to tell the truth and protects us from lies. God knows when we lie to Him or to others. This means, more importantly, that our inner strength and protection come from God's truth.

"But we have renounced the hidden things of shame, not walking in craftiness, nor handling the word of God deceitfully, but by manifestation of the truth commending ourselves to every man's conscience in the sight of God." II Corinthians 4:2

The Breastplate of Righteousness – protects the heart and helps us to know who we are in Christ.

"For the Lord God is a sun and shield; The Lord will give grace and glory; No good thing will He withhold From those who walk uprightly." Psalm 84:11

The Sandals of Peace – are sandals that are shod with the preparation of the gospel of peace. This helps us to walk in God's ways and keep us from stumbling because we are properly clad.

"And the peace of God, which surpasses all understanding, will guard your hearts and minds through Christ Jesus." Philippians 4:7

The Sword of the Spirit – is the Bible. We should memorize scripture. God likes us to speak His scriptures back to Him when we are praying, reminding Him of what His word says and what His promises are to us. As we quote them, they strengthen us and run the enemy off.

"For the word of God is living and powerful, and sharper than any two-edged sword, piercing even to the division of soul and spirit, and of joints and marrow, and is a discerner of the thoughts and intents of the heart." Hebrews 4:12

The Helmet of Salvation – protects us from bad thoughts. We are made stronger by reading God's word and meditating on it during the day. When negative situations befall us during the day, instead of reacting to the situation, we should think of a scripture that applies and meditate on that scripture instead.

"Therefore, you shall lay up these words of mine in your heart and in your soul, and bind them as a sign on your hand, and they shall be as frontlets between your eyes." Deuteronomy 11:18

The Shield of Faith – lets us know God is always with us, even when things are going wrong and we cannot see Him working. That is when our faith should rise, and we should be determined to know God is at work for us and is there to help us defeat our foes. Just as a physical shield protects the body, when used correctly, our faith under fire protects the whole person from the fiery darts of the wicked.

"Let us hold fast the confession of our hope without wavering; for He who promised is faithful." Hebrews 10:23

We should come to God in prayer and ask Him to help us throughout the day. He is always there for us, yearning to help His children.

Now as we journey through this book, I want to show who God is and how He works in the lives of His children through prayer.

Let's start at the beginning!

2

HOW SIN AFFECTED MANKIND

"In the beginning God created the heavens and the earth." Genesis 1:1

God in all His love, power and majesty created the world in which we exist. As an artist would take a canvas and create, so did our Creator. Every tree, every flower, every mountain or ocean, God spoke into existence. Using His imagination, He created every animal large and small. Only then did He create man in His image and name him Adam.

After God created Adam, He placed him in the Garden of Eden to be the caretaker. Adam was created to rule under God. The Garden of Eden was more beautiful than we could ever imagine with every precious stone.

"You were in Eden, the garden of God; Every precious stone was your covering: The sardius, topaz, and diamond, Beryl, onyx, and jasper, Sapphire, turquoise, and emerald with gold." Ezekiel 28:13

The garden was full of animals, flowers and every kind of tree. The flowers were pleasing to the eye and the trees were good for food. In the middle of the garden flowed a river which was there to water it.

"In the middle of the garden grew the Tree of Life and the Tree of the Knowledge of the Good and Evil. God told Adam he could eat from any tree in the garden except the Tree of the Knowledge of the Good and Evil. And if he did eat from this tree he would die." Genesis 2:9 & Genesis 2:16-17

The Lord did not want Adam to be alone, so He caused Adam to fall into a deep sleep and took one of his ribs and made a woman from it. When Adam awoke, he saw the woman and named her Eve, because she was the Mother of all living things.

There was no sin in the Garden of Eden at this time. Adam and Eve were sinless.

Along came the serpent. He was sly and devious. He convinced Eve that she could eat from the Tree of the Knowledge of Good and Evil. Eve ate a piece of fruit from the tree and then gave some to Adam. Satan convinced Eve that God had not meant that they would die if they ate from the tree, but that their eyes would be opened and that they would be like God.

After they ate some of the fruit, their eyes were opened and they realized they were naked. They had not known this before and were so ashamed. They realized what they had done was wrong, but it was too late. They could not undo the facts. They had sinned!

Soon they heard God walking in the garden. He called out for Adam, "Where are you Adam?"

Adam answered God. He said, "I heard Your voice in the garden and was afraid because I was naked and I hid myself." Genesis 3:10

God said, "Who told you that you were naked? Have you eaten from the tree of which I commanded you that you should not eat?" Genesis 3:11

Even though God asked Adam this question, He knew the answer because God is an all-knowing God. He wanted Adam to confess to Him what he had done.

Adam said, "The woman whom you gave to be with me, she gave me of the tree, and I ate." Genesis 3:12

Eve said, "The serpent deceived me, and I ate." Genesis 3:13

Eve was deceived by Satan. Adam blamed God and Eve, and Eve blamed the serpent. The guilt, fear, worthlessness and shame they were feeling had come from Satan. Satan is always there to make us feel guilty, fearful, unworthy, and ashamed or whatever the case may be. We all have felt the same kinds of feelings Adam and Eve felt, because we all have sinned. Satan is always there to accuse.

Adam had disobeyed God, and by doing so, he surrendered to Satan the authority to rule the earth that God had given to man.

God said, "I will put enmity Between you and the woman, And between your seed and her Seed; He shall bruise your head, And you shall lie in wait and bruise His heel." Genesis 3:15

To "bruise the head" symbolizes a weakening of authority. God had said that the Offspring (Jesus) will take away Satan's authority. Satan will bruise Jesus' heel (afflict His body-both on the cross and by afflicting mankind.) [1]

They had done the one thing God had asked them not to do. How many times have we committed sin and then realized we had allowed Satan to deceive us?

We may not be guilty of eating a forbidden fruit, but we are all guilty of sin.

"If we say that we have no sin, we deceive ourselves, and the truth is not in us. If we confess our sins, He is faithful and just to forgive us our sins and to cleanse us from all unrighteousness." 1 John 1:8-9

"Also for Adam and his wife, the Lord God made tunics of skin, and clothed them." Genesis 3:21

Let's reflect on this tunic of skin. To have the skin, there had to have been an animal. Adam and Eve had to make atonement for their sin before they left the Garden of Eden. Atonement requires blood as a covering for sin. Consequently, the animal blood was used.

"For the life of the flesh is in the blood, and I have given it to you upon the altar to make atonement for your souls; for it is the blood that makes atonement for the soul." Leviticus 17:11

This verse is talking about the sacrifice made for the sins of the Israelites, but I feel that it could very well apply in the case of Adam and Eve also. The only price for sin that God will accept is blood. The sacrifice of blood means one life is given for another. Atonement means "make amends with God."

After Adam and Eve sinned, everything changed. Their sin warped everything God had created. It affected the earth, the animals, their lives and all living things. That is what sin does; it affects everything, even the entire human race. The intrusion of sin made it impossible for mankind to worship God in the Garden of Eden. Through blood sacrifices atonement was made. Jesus was the blood sacrifice for our sins.

"For all have sinned and fall short of the glory of God." Romans 3:23

The Garden of Eden was considered "holy" because of God's presence in the garden. Therefore, there could be no sin in the garden. God wanted to make a sanctuary where He could come and commune with His creation. The Garden of Eden was holy ground, patterned after the Temple in Heaven.

According to history, the Garden of Eden was on a higher elevation (a mountain) with four rivers flowing downward out of the garden. The four rivers were facing eastward.

"So He drove out the man; and He placed cherubim at the east of the garden of Eden, and a flaming sword which turned every way, to guard the way to the tree of life." Genesis 3:24

God put the cherubim (a category of angels) and the flaming sword at the entrance, so no one could enter the Garden of Eden again, and no one could go west to the Tree of Life.

When Adam and Eve left the Garden of Eden, they had many hardships, but one of God's promises is that He will never leave us nor forsake us.

Adam and Eve had two sons named Cain and Abel. Abel was a herdsman and had given God the firstborn of his flock for a sin offering. God accepted Abel's offering for his sin. Cain worked the soil and gave God some of the fruit of the soil, as a sin offering. God did not accept Cain's offering because his offering did not signify the blood atonement that was needed for a sin offering. Cain became jealous and was furious with Abel, so Cain killed Abel.

God's judgment now stood between fallen man and the Garden of Eden. Man can have access to the Tree of Life only through Christ's redemption.

Redemption means being bought with a price and delivered from sin. Have you been redeemed or have you realized the need for a Redeemer?

GOD'S FORGIVENESS

Sin and corruption will destroy our lives
Through repentance and forgiveness
We can become wise
He only asks that we come by faith
Longing to give us His mercy and grace
He gives freely to all who truly believe
Willing to bow down and eager to please

3

BLESSINGS FROM
THE FATHER

The Lord wants to bless us. He wants to bless us through our prayers, our work, our home, and our family. God is a giving God. He longs to give us the desires of our heart.

"Delight yourself also in the Lord, and He shall give you the desires of your heart." Psalm 37:4

God wants to bless us, and one of the ways He does this is through our prayers. The more we pray, the more God blesses. He wants us to come to Him with our petitions.

"Ask, and it will be given to you; seek, and you will find; knock, and it will be opened to you. For everyone who asks receives, and he who seeks finds, and to him who knocks it will be opened." Matthew 7:7-8

We have not, because we ask not. God wants to open doors for us that no one else can open. He wants us to ask and seek His face, so He can bless us.

Can God bless us anyway if we don't pray? Of course He can and He does. Life is a blessing. When we get up in the morning, we are blessed. Prayer releases blessings. He wants us to come to Him, as we do our earthly father, because He is our Father. Anyone who has accepted Christ as his Savior has God as his Father. Who is this God, this Father to whom we are to pray?

Let me explain: the Trinity is the three Persons of the Christian Godhead (Father, Son, and Holy Spirit).

God, the Father, is our Heavenly Father.

God, the Son, is the Heavenly Father's Son. He is Jesus Christ, who came to earth and died for our sins on the cross of Calvary.

The Holy Spirit is the Spirit of God that dwells in us. His job is to guide, lead and teach us, after we have accepted Jesus as our Savior.

We come to God the Father through Jesus Christ His Son, the second person of the Trinity. Jesus Christ is our Advocate (our go-between) to God the Father. Jesus is the High Priest in Heaven making intercession for us to His Father.

"Seeing then that we have a great High Priest who has passed through the heavens, Jesus the Son of God, let us hold fast our confession. For we do not have a High Priest who cannot sympathize with our weaknesses, but was in all points tempted as we are, yet without sin. Let us therefore come boldly to the throne of grace that we may obtain mercy and find grace in our time of need." Hebrews 4:14-16

Satan is always there to accuse us and condemn us, but Jesus is there making intercession for us. Jesus is a special Blessing, come down from God.

Without God, our life is empty and without purpose. But, with God, we can have a fulfilled life and a hope of an eternal home. But we can only have God if we accept Jesus and His sacrifice. But, how do we do that? The scripture makes it simple.

To be saved, we have to come by faith and believe Jesus died on the cross and arose again after three days.

"If you confess with your mouth the Lord Jesus and believe in your heart that God raised him from the dead, you will be saved. For with the heart one believes unto righteousness, and with the mouth confession is made unto salvation." Romans 10:9-10

Jesus will hear your prayer and go to the Father on your behalf, and God will save you.

Jesus said, "I am the Way, the Truth, and the Life. No one comes to the Father except through Me." John 14:6

This is the first prayer one needs to pray. Confessing faith and belief in what Jesus did gives a person the right to bring his petitions to God.

Jesus has bridged the gap between us and God. Sin divides us from God, but God has opened the door of Heaven to you by way of His Son, Jesus Christ.

"Therefore, He is also able to save to the utter-most those who come to God through Him, since

He always lives to make intercession for them." Hebrews 7:25

"For such a High Priest was fitting for us, who is holy, blameless, undefiled, separated from sinners, and has become higher than the heavens; who does not need daily, as those high priests, to offer up sacrifices, first for His own sins and then for the people's, for this He did once for all when He offered up Himself." Hebrews 7:26-27

There are times when we go to God and we don't know how to pray. That is when the Holy Spirit, third Person of the Trinity, intercedes for us. Then God hears what we are really asking from our hearts, even though we may not know. But the Holy Spirit knows what we need before we ask.

Why do we need an Intercessor? Why do we need Jesus? Because God cannot look on sin! We can only approach God through a Mediator, which is Jesus Christ. He is without sin, so God can look on Him.

Even though, as a Christian, we have been washed by the blood of the Lamb, we need daily cleansing. So, we come daily through Christ His Son. There is no other way to approach God except through His Son, Jesus Christ.

This should tell us of the righteousness of God and the wickedness of sin. There is not one of us without a need to come to the mercy seat of God to be forgiven for our sin. God is always full of compassion, mercy and grace. Jesus is always praying for us day and night, never ceasing on our behalf. That is pure love.

"Jesus gave Himself for our sins, that He might deliver us from this present evil age, according to the will of our God and Father." Galatians 1:4

Jesus often went to a solitary place to pray. He went before God, bringing His petitions, asking for guidance, praising God's name, and thanking Him for all He had done. As He went to different towns to preach, heal the sick, calm the storms, cast out demons or whatever the task, He went to God in solitude, first and foremost. He set the example for us in our daily walk.

"Now in the morning, having raised a long while before daylight, He went out and departed to a solitary place; and there He prayed." Mark 1:35

When Jesus was on earth, His life was inundated with prayer. Jesus was the greatest Prayer Warrior of all time.

"When He offered up prayers of supplication, with vehement cries and tears to Him who was able to save Him from death, and was heard because of His Godly fear, though He was a Son, yet He learned obedience by the things which He suffered." Hebrews 5:7

Jesus' prayers unleashed the Power of God. We can have the same power, if we will but go to God in prayer. God wants us to come to Him alone and find solace. As we come to God, we talk to Him as if we were talking to a friend. He wants to hear our voice. As we talk to God, we should tell Him how we love Him and want to be more like Him. We should never feel that we are so close to God that we have no reason to pray. That is one of Satan's snares, and that is when we will fall because of foolish pride. If Jesus felt the need to pray, so should we!

We should be greatly honored to have the High Priest interceding on our behalf.

Prayer is a privilege. As we come to God, we should intercede for others as well as ourselves. This is intercessory prayer. We all have a need for prayer, and we should want to intercede for each other.

Each of us needs to set aside a time to pray every day. We need to guard and protect it, or Satan will see that we won't have time for prayer.

We may say, "I don't have time to pray; I'm too busy." The busier we are, the more we need to pray. We can get up earlier in the morning or stay up later for prayer. God wants to hear from us, and we need to hear from God. If we feel God is not answering our prayers, we need to make sure our heart is right before God. We need to ask forgiveness for all our sins, naming them, one by one, as we think of them. God will reveal any hidden sin in our life, if we ask. We can talk to God and watch Him work. Prayer draws us closer to God. If we do not pray, we lose our communication with God; we lose our faith. We lose our love for other people, and we lose the kind of fellowship that we need with others. Then, we are frustrated and aggravated, and Satan takes over.

The more we know God, the more desperate we are for God. If we feel we have no need for God, Satan is deceiving us. Sin divides us from God. Satan wants us to feel that we are self-sufficient and that we are in control of our life. But the truth is if God is not in control of our life, Satan is controlling us.

"The Lord is far from the wicked, But He hears the prayer of the righteous." Proverbs 15:29

God is waiting for an invitation to work in us and through us. It's a thrill to see God work in our lives. We must allow God to take control of our life, and we will do things we never thought possible. With God all things are possible.

If we feel we are unworthy to pray, or have committed too big a sin, or are too hurt to pray, Jesus is already interceding on our behalf. Jesus intercedes for God's children day and night. God wants to hear from each one of us. God's word says if we have the faith of a mustard seed we can move mountains. Think what God could accomplish through us, if we would but go to Him with all our petitions, believing, He would move mountains on our behalf.

If we feel God will not forgive us of our sin, God is not condemning us; we must forgive ourselves. A lot of people cannot forgive themselves of things they have done in the past. If you come to God in prayer with a humble heart and ask forgiveness for your sin, God will forgive you. Therefore, if God will forgive you of your sin, then you should forgive yourself.

"There is therefore now no condemnation to those who are in Christ Jesus, who do not walk according to the flesh, but according to the Spirit. For the law of the Spirit of life in Christ Jesus has made me free from the law of sin and death. For what the law could not do in that it was weak through the flesh. God did by sending His own Son in the likeness of sinful flesh, on account of sin: He condemned sin in the flesh, that the righteous requirement of the law might be fulfilled in us who do not walk according to the flesh, but according to the spirit." Romans 8:1-4

My sin is as far from me as the East is from the West, and God forgets it when I ask forgiveness.

When we sin, it breaks the flow of God's Power, so as we recognize our sin throughout the day, we need to continue to ask forgiveness. Then God will hear our prayers and answer.

If we are not overcoming our trials here on earth, it is because of a lack of prayer. How many answers to prayers do we miss because we are not praying or listening to God? We need to go to the Mercy Seat and commune with God daily.

Prayer is the backbone of any individual, family unit, or church. Without prayer, none of us can function as we should. When we pray, the angels start to work on our behalf. We need to ask for supernatural favor from God. He can do more than we can ever imagine.

Jesus was the perfect sacrificial Lamb who knew no sin. As He went to the Garden of Gethsemane to pray, He was horrified at the thought of the sin he was to bear for all mankind.

"For He made Him who knew no sin to be sin for us, that we might become the righteousness of God in Him." II Corinthians 5:21

As He hung on the cross, we cannot fathom the pain and agony He went through so that we could be free from hell. The way of the Cross is the way to victory. Jesus broke the chains and set us free. With Him we are free indeed.

The Way of the Cross leads Home.

If you would like to have a Savior, Redeemer and Friend, I suggest that you pray a prayer similar to this:

Heavenly Father,

I come to You today believing that Your Son (Jesus Christ) died on the Cross for my sin and arose again after three days. I am asking You to forgive me of my sin and that You would save me so I can spend all eternity with You in Heaven, as well as live a life of victory here on earth.

Thank You for saving me. Thank You for the Cross and for Your Son who shed His blood and was the sacrificial Lamb who died in my place.

Amen!

If you have prayed this prayer sincerely, you are now one of God's children. May God bless your life and work in you and through you, to bring glory to God and to help further His Kingdom. The key to success in your life is to be obedient to God. God loves you and wants what is best for you. He will never fail you.

BLESSINGS FROM GOD

Infinite wisdom, worthy and true
Blessings from God, sent especially to you
He in His power, He in His name,
Only want glory from you, not shame

4

ACCEPTANCE AND DELIVERANCE

God always makes a covenant (agreement) with His people. Our covenant with God is through His Son Jesus Christ.

After Noah built the ark and the flood came, God spoke to Noah and his sons and said there would never be another flood to destroy the earth. God said He was sending a sign from heaven which is the rainbow in the clouds.

God said, "And as for Me, behold, I establish My covenant with you, and with your descendants after you, and with every living creature that is with you: the birds, the cattle, and every beast of the earth with you, of all that go out of the ark, every beast of the earth. I set My rainbow in the cloud and it shall be for the sign of the covenant between Me and the earth." Genesis 9:9 & Genesis 9:13

God also made a covenant with Abram: "As for Me, behold, My covenant is with you, and you shall be a father to many nations. No longer shall your name be called Abram, but your name shall be Abraham; for I have made you a father of many nations." Genesis 17:4-5

A covenant was made with Moses and the Israelites. "These are the words of the covenant which the Lord commanded Moses to make with the children of Israel in the land of Moab, besides the covenant which He made with them in Horeb." Deuteronomy 29:1

God had taken the Israelites out of Egyptian bondage. They had been slaves to the Egyptians and had been treated harshly by Pharaoh. God delivered them from Egypt and took them into the wilderness for forty years. Through all the trials, God was faithful. He had furnished Israel with manna from Heaven daily. Their clothes and shoes had never worn out; they conquered in battles against their enemies, and God parted the Red Sea so they could cross over before their enemy could defeat them.

In return, God had asked them to enter into a covenant to have no other gods before them, to love, serve and obey His commandments. If they would do as God commanded them, He would bless them and allow them to enter into the Promised Land.

Let's go on a journey with Moses and the Israelites and see how God delivered them from bondage from the Egyptians and how they entered into the covenant with God.

Moses' parents were named Amram and Jacobed. Both parents of Moses were descendants of Levi, one of the tribes of Israel.

Moses was born a beautiful child and lived in his parents' home, hidden for the first three months. Pharaoh had instructed the midwives to kill all the male babies three months old or younger because he was afraid the Israelites would grow in number and take control of the government. That is why Moses had to be hidden the first three months of his life.

"But when she could no longer hide him, she took an ark of bulrushes for him, daubed it with asphalt and pitch, put the child in it, and laid it in the reeds by the river's bank." Exodus 2:3

The daughter of Pharaoh came to bathe in the river. She saw the babe and asked her maid servant, Miriam, Moses' older sister, to take him and get a nurse for him. Miriam called Jacobed, their mother, and a Hebrew, to come and care for him.

"Then Pharaoh's daughter said to her, take this child and nurse him for me, and I will give you your wages." Exodus 2:9

Jacobed got to care for her own son and got paid for it. What mother wouldn't like that? Jacobed and Amram raised him long enough to make a good impression and give him the basic training he needed. Amram and Jacobed were God-fearing parents and taught Moses accordingly. Amram had a dream that Moses would someday deliver the Israelites out of Egypt. They also remembered the covenant

God had given to Abraham and the promise that the Israelites would be delivered from Egypt in the fourth generation.

Pharaoh's daughter saw Moses as her heir to the throne and took him as her own son, naming him Moses, which means "drawn out," particularly out of the water. Moses was trained as a leader in the military, as well as in wisdom and the knowledge of the Egyptian culture, to be the heir to the throne of Egypt.

As Moses grew older, he never forgot his own people, even though he lived in a palace, had claim to all the wealth, culture and possessions of Egypt and lived under Pharaoh's rule. He could never accept Pharaoh's daughter as his mother and refused to be called her son.

After he was grown, he killed an Egyptian who was beating one of the Hebrew people. Pharaoh heard about this and wanted to kill Moses, so Moses fled for his life, forsaking Egypt.

He fled to Midian and married the daughter of a priest. While there, Moses became a shepherd and helped with his father's-in-law herd.

"He led the flock to the back of the desert, and came to Horeb, the mountain of God." The Angel of the Lord appeared to him in a flame of fire from the midst of a bush. So he looked, and behold, the bush was burning with fire, but the bush was not consumed. Then Moses said, "I will now turn aside and see this great sight, why the bush does not burn." So when the Lord saw that he turned aside to look, God called to him from the midst of the bush and said, "Moses, Moses!"

And he said, "Here I am."

Then He said, "Do not draw near this place. Take your sandals off your feet, for the place where you stand is holy ground." Moreover He said, "I am the God of your Father – the God of Abraham, the God of Isaac, and the God of Jacob. And Moses hid his face, for he was afraid to look upon God.

And the Lord said, "I have surely seen the oppression of my people who are in Egypt, and have heard their cry because of their taskmasters, for I know their sorrow. So I have come down to deliver them from the hand of the Egyptians and to bring them up from that land to a good and large land, to a land flowing with milk and honey." Exodus 3:1-8

God wanted to send Moses back to Pharaoh to ask Pharaoh to allow the Israelites to leave Egypt. God told Moses that He would be with him, and that when he brought the Israelites back, he would serve Him on that mountain.

Moses asked God, "Who shall I say sent me?" God said to say, "I AM WHO I AM." The "I AM" has sent you to the Israelites." Exodus 3:14

Moses went back to Egypt, asking for his people. God sent Aaron, Moses' brother, to go with him. They went to all the elders of the Israelites and told them what God had said. The Israelites believed them and bowed and worshiped God.

Next, they went to Pharaoh and asked for him to allow the Israelites to leave Egypt. Pharaoh refused and instead made them work harder. In the first five plagues Pharaoh hardened his own heart. In the sixth through tenth plague, God confirmed Pharaoh's willful action as He had told Moses He would do. (Exodus 4:21)

God sent several plagues to the land of Egypt, showing His Mighty Power and the testing of Israel's faith. The plagues also showed that God would not be mocked and that He would execute judgment on the person who hardens his heart. God loved Israel even though He knew they were worshiping pagan gods. He wanted to be their One True God. None of these plagues came on the Israelites, only the Egyptians.

The first plague was that God turned the water to blood. There was no water to drink, and all the fish died and the water began to stink. But Pharaoh hardened his heart, refusing to let the Israelites go.

The second plague was frogs. There were frogs in their beds, rivers, on the land, in their homes and on the people. Everywhere they looked there were frogs. Still, Pharaoh hardened his heart.

The third plague was lice. There were lice on every man and animal. Pharaoh still would not allow the Israelites to go with Moses.

The fourth plague was flies. There were swarms of flies on the Egyptians, their homes, their animals and servants. There were flies on the ground and the land was corrupt because of the flies. But Pharaoh's heart was still hardened, and he would not allow the Israelites to go with Moses.

The fifth plague was pestilence on the livestock of the Egyptians. All the livestock of the Egyptians died, but God allowed the livestock of Israel to live. But, again, Pharaoh hardened his heart.

The sixth plague was boils. God told Moses and Aaron to take handfuls of ashes from the furnaces and scatter it toward the heavens as Pharaoh was watching. This caused boils to break out on all the people and animals. Pharaoh continued to hardened his heart and not allow the Israelites to leave Egypt.

The seventh plague was hail. There was hail, fire and thunder in all the land of Egypt. This time Pharaoh sent for Moses and admitted to him that the earth was God's and that he and his people had sinned against God. He told Moses that Israel could leave Egypt, but when the hail, fire and thunder stopped, he hardened his heart again and would not allow Israel to go with Moses.

So God allowed the eighth plague, which was locusts, to come and eat every herb of the land that the hail had not destroyed. By this time, the land was extremely desolate. The locusts covered Egypt. Pharaoh sent for Moses again. He admitted that he had sinned again, and God turned a strong wind to Egypt, and the entire locusts swarm went into the Red sea. Again Pharaoh hardened his heart.

God allowed yet another plague to come against Egypt. For three days, there was total darkness in all the land of Egypt. No one could see anything or anyone. God told Moses to prepare Israel for the Passover, which would protect them from the final plague.

God said he would go into the land of Egypt at midnight, and all of the firstborn of Pharaoh, the Egyptians and their animals would die. Moses was to go to the people of Israel and tell them to take a lamb or goat without blemish and kill it at twilight. They were to take some of the blood and put it on the doorpost and lintels.

"When God passed over the land of Egypt, He would see the blood on the doorpost and He would pass over them. Therefore, He would not kill any of the Israelites' firstborn." (Exodus 12:13)

God did not protect Israel because He loved them more than the Egyptians, but because they were His children. God's grace and mercy are always sufficient for His children. The Exodus of Israel from Egypt was an intense conflict between God and Satan. God could have killed Pharaoh and taken the Israelites, but instead He gave Pharaoh every chance to repent. This shows God's love for Pharaoh and the Egyptians.

God loves us just as much as He did the Israelites, Egyptians and Pharaoh. And we also need God's grace and mercy. We are just as sinful as the Israelites or the Egyptians. What other gods (false idols) do we serve? Could it be money, a fancy car, a relationship, or our job? Anything that we put above God is an idol! God wants our undivided attention. He wants to be our one and only true God, and He wants us to serve Him and Him alone. As God gave Pharaoh every chance, He also gives us every chance for repentance. God is patient with us, even when we don't deserve it. This shows His awesome love for us.

After the Passover, there was much sorrow in the land of Egypt. Every household was affected.

Pharaoh had no choice but to allow the children of Israel to go with Moses. The Israelites had been slaves to the Egyptians for four hundred thirty years.

When they left Egypt, they took their clothing, their flocks and herds, silver and gold. There were twelve tribes in all, which were six hundred thousand men on foot besides children. God led the people by orderly ranks out of Egypt. The twelve tribes were named Dan, Asher, Nephtali, Judah, Zebulah, Issachar, Reuben, Gad, Simeon, Ephraim, Benjamin, and Manasseh.

"The Lord went before them by day in a pillar of cloud to lead the way, and by night in a pillar of fire to give them light, so as to go by day and night." Exodus 13:21

Pharaoh and his army pursued the Israelites and were ready for battle. "God told Moses to lift his rod and stretch out his hand over the Red Sea and He would part the waters so Israel could cross over the sea. There was a wall of water on both sides. God caused the wind to blow all night to dry the ground so Israel could cross over. The Israelites crossed the sea and then God told Moses to stretch his hand across the sea and the waters would go back over the Egyptians. All the Egyptians, horses and chariots that pursued Israel died in the Red sea." Exodus 14:15-23

All of Israel saw the great work of the Lord and accepted Moses as a great leader. Moses progressed with faith, boldness and power. He acted in obedience and relied on God and not himself. He had the rod of a shepherd and was God's ambassador, with God's infinite power.

But what does this have to do with people today? As God took the Israelites out of Egyptian bondage, He took them on a longer route to protect, train, and tests them. He does the same with us. God has a plan for every one of our lives. He watches every aspect of our lives, protecting us from Satan's snares, training us to do His will and testing us through trials.

Look at Moses' life. God was training him from the time he was born. It was not by chance that Moses ended up living at Pharaoh's palace. And it was not by chance that Moses was trained to be heir to the throne of Egypt, but God had another plan. If we reflect on Moses' life and see how God trained him as a leader, we will also see how He trained him in a different way than what was planned by man. Sometimes we don't understand things that happen in life, but God is in control of the "Big Picture." It is for our benefit to learn from the experiences of life. When we have trials, they can strengthen our faith, build character, and allow us to see God's power working on our behalf.

As we seek God's face on all our decisions, the thought may come, "When I pray, I don't hear God speak to me." Sometimes we have to wait for God to speak. In our quiet time, we need to listen for God. We need to ask Him for guidance and direction. As we wait, He will turn our pride into humility and doubt into faith, or He may allow us to go through a conflict to watch us grow.

As in this story, Pharaoh's stubborn pride would not allow Moses to take Israel out of Egypt. Satan had a hold on Pharaoh through his pride, but he was blinded to the fact. How many times have we allowed Satan to have a hold on us? Could it be through unforgiveness, selfishness, arrogance, pride or any number of sins? We need to self-check ourselves daily to see any area we have given over to Satan and ask forgiveness from God.

As Moses stood before God, let us look at his leadership qualities, his faithfulness, obedience, dependency upon God, and the miracles that were performed because of all these qualities. We are in the same position as Moses. We may not be leading Israel to the Promised Land, but we have our own responsibilities, and need to be just as loyal to God as Moses. We need to be loyal with our life, our conduct and our finances. We need to stay close to God through prayer. We need to be good stewards with all God entrusts us to, asking for wisdom, knowledge and discernment.

The Israelites had been delivered from Egypt by God and separated from Egypt by the parting of the Red Sea. They had walked by faith, and God wanted to continue to teach them; this is why He took them to the desert on their way.

We may feel as if we are walking through a desert sometimes too; but if we are, it is because God is working in us and wants us to learn from our experience. If we don't know what we are supposed to be learning, we can ask God to show us. It may be faith, humility, grace, patience, kindness, or a number of other things. But we can be sure God is always teaching us through our trials.

When we give our life to God, completely, He will do above and beyond, more than we could imagine!

Yes, God delivered His people then, and He desires to deliver us today from the enemy. We can pray for His deliverance in every area of our life. Are we in bondage anywhere? He will show us if we ask Him! Just as the people had to be willing to leave Egypt, we have to be willing for Him to remove every trace of bondage/addiction/sin from our own life. We have to be willing to place our lives in His hands, even as the Israelites placed their lives in the hands of Moses. And we have to be willing for God to take as much time as He needs to do His finished work in our lives. To God is the glory, now and forevermore!

Jesus said everything is based on our having faith in Him. That is the way we enter into Covenant with Him. He will do the work in us; our part is to believe! What a deal! What an agreement! What a covenant!

Praise His Name!

5

SHEKINAH GLORY
(DWELLING IN THE MAJESTY AND PRESENCE OF GOD)

For centuries, Israel had lived in the cities and on fertile farm land in Egypt. What a contrast the wilderness was compared to their previous habitation! The wilderness was like a desert, and there was no way the Israelites could provide for themselves. Now, they had to depend on Moses. After crossing the Red Sea, they started complaining to Moses and complaining to each other about Moses because they didn't know what they would eat or drink. Remember, they had lived a life of slavery, totally dependent on Pharaoh. Now, Moses went to God on their behalf; and God, rather than Pharaoh, provided for their physical needs. Then as now, God was much more interested in having a relationship with them. God is always more interested in having a family than slaves.

The Israelites had now come to the wilderness and were camped before Mt. Sinai. Moses went up the mountain to God and the Lord called to him saying to tell the children of Israel:

"You have seen what I did to the Egyptians, and how I bore you on eagles' wings and brought you to Myself. Now therefore, if you will indeed obey My voice and keep My covenant, then you shall be a special treasure to Me above all the people; for all the earth is Mine. And you shall be to Me a kingdom of priests and a holy nation. These are the words which you shall speak to the children of Israel." Exodus 19:4-6

Moses came back down and called all the elders of the people and told them what God had said. They answered in unison, vowing to do all the Lord had told them. So Moses returned to the mountain and told God what the people had said.

And the Lord said to Moses, "Behold, I come to you in the thick cloud, that the people may hear when I speak with you, and believe you forever." Exodus 19:9

Then the Lord told Moses to go to the people and consecrate them (or declare them sacred) for two days and tell them to wash their clothes. On the third day, the Lord will come down the mountain in the sight of all the people. The people are not to go up the mountain or even touch the base of the mountain, or they will be put to death.

In the morning of the third day, thunder and lightning sounded loudly and a thick cloud was on the mountain, and a trumpet sounded so loud that everyone trembled. Moses brought all the people near the mountain to meet with God. The mountain was completely engulfed in smoke, because the Lord descended upon it in fire. The smoke ascended like the smoke of a furnace, and the whole mountain quaked. The trumpet blast became longer, louder and louder. Moses spoke, and God answered him. The Lord came down on top of the mountain and called Moses up to the mountain. God told him to go back down and get Aaron, the High Priest, but not to bring any other priest or anyone else up the mountain. So Moses followed God's orders.

"And God spoke all these words to the people saying:

I am the Lord your God, who brought you out of Egypt, out of the house of bondage.

You shall have no other gods before me.

You shall not make for yourself a carved image.

You shall not take the name of the Lord your God in vain, for the Lord will not hold him guiltless who takes His name in vain.

Remember the Sabbath day to keep it holy.

Honor your father and your mother.

You shall not murder.

You shall not commit adultery.

You shall not steal.

You shall not bear false witness against your neighbor.

You shall not covet your neighbor's house, nor anything that is your neighbor's." Exodus 20:1-17

The above scripture contains the Ten Commandments that God gave to Moses on the mountain for Israel. These Commandments were and are the moral guidelines that God gave Israel to live by, guidelines that are still applicable today. God gave the Israelites directions for living a good and moral life.

When the people witnessed the thundering and lightning, the sound of the trumpet, and the mountain smoking, they trembled while standing and watching from afar. They were scared because God had spoken. They told Moses that they would listen to him, but they didn't want to hear from God because they were afraid of Him, afraid they would die. Moses told them that God was testing them and that God wanted them to fear Him to prevent sin. Then Moses went to God, and the Lord told Moses He did not want Israel to make for themselves any gods of silver or gold, but to build an altar of earth to make burnt offerings and peace offerings.

Later, Moses went up on Mt. Sinai again, but he left Aaron and Hur (Priests) to take care of the people. A cloud covered the mountain, and the glory of the Lord settled on it. The Israelites were at the bottom of the mountain, and to them, the glory of the Lord looked like a consuming fire on top of the mountain. Moses entered the cloud and stayed there forty days and forty nights with God. (Exodus 24:15-18)

While Moses was with God, he was given the directions for the Tabernacle. Also, God told him the people had corrupted themselves and were worshiping a false idol, and had even made a sacrifice to it. Moses begged God not to destroy the Israelites, but to show them mercy. So God relented from harming Israel, because of Moses.

When Moses returned to the people, he carried with him the two tablets of stone, on which God had written the Commandments. And when he came down the mountain, he saw that Israel was worshiping a false idol, made by Aaron. It was a golden calf made from the gold jewelry of the wives, sons and daughters of Israel. Moses had been gone so long the people didn't know what happened to him, and had asked Aaron to make them a god.

As Moses came near the camp and heard the noise of the people, seeing them dancing, and seeing the golden calf (their false idol), he could see that the people were out of control. He was furious and broke the tablets of stone at the foot of the mountain. He took the calf and burned it in the fire, then he ground it into ashes, and scattered the ashes on the water, and then made the children of Israel drink it. Moses saw the people were not repentant for what they had done.

Moses was not shy about exacting punishment for their behavior, and he stood at the entrance of the camp, asking those who were on the Lord's side to come to him. The sons of Levi came to him. And he told them to draw their swords and go in and out from entrance to entrance of the camp and kill his brother, every man his companion, and every man his neighbor. About three thousand men died that day. More would have died, had they not chosen to stand with Moses. (Exodus 32:26-28)

Moses told the people they had sinned again and promised to go to the Lord on their behalf. So, he went again to God to make atonement for their sins. Moses said to God,

"If you will, forgive their sin-but if not, I pray, blot me out of your book which you have written." Exodus 32:32

Moses, as their mediator, now made urgent intercession for the people of Israel. He offered himself as the sacrifice for their sin, but God did not accept the offering of Moses on Israel's behalf. Each individual must be held responsible for his own sin. Moses predated Jesus, and no one can atone for another except Jesus, who died once for all, on the cross, to atone for our sins.

As we look back at the overall picture, we see the Israelites had lived in Egypt for over four hundred years and were so much a part of the world system that it could be said, "The world was in them." This did not help, but rather hurt, when God began separating them from the world. They didn't recognize the need to change, and they put little or no stock in what God said. They were easily swayed by the worldly thoughts and attitudes and the worldly way of doing things. The word "faith" was probably not even in their vocabulary. Prayer, as we know it today, probably did not exist either.

But, remember this was after the time of Abraham, Isaac, Jacob and Joseph. The knowledge of God and faith in God had been a part of their life at one time.

But, their years of bondage in Egypt had caused many to be almost indistinguishable from the world.

Are we any different than the Israelites? I don't think so! How many times have we forsaken God in times of difficulty and stress? How many times have we put other things before God, making those things into false idols, and worshiped our false idols instead of God? And how many times have we been influenced more by those around us than by God?

Moses loved the Israelites with an unconditional love. He went up the mountain on behalf of the Israelites many times to dissuade God from destroying Israel. How many times has Jesus done the same for us, going before God on our behalf, asking God to give us one more chance?

Moses had compassion and a love for Israel that only God could have given him. As Israel's advocate, Moses spent hours in defense of and care for Israel. Jesus, our Advocate, prays day and night on our behalf, before God.

Moses was willing to sacrifice his life for his people. Jesus did sacrifice His life for (us) His people. Now that is love!

When we talk about the Israelites in the wilderness, we are talking about millions of people for a period of forty years. There were twelve tribes in all, with all kinds of personalities, likes and dislikes. Murmuring and complaining about God, complaining about Moses and complaining about their situation were part of their life. They worshiped false idols; they were difficult to get along with; they accused Moses of taking them into the wilderness to die. And this was all on a good day. And no doubt whatever sin we can imagine was taking place. Moses had to deal with this daily, had to keep asking God to forgive Israel over and over again, and no doubt had to ask for wisdom for himself. Through all of this, Moses maintained a great love for these people. How can this be? How could he continue to love these people, who were so wicked? God, continually, gave him a love for Israel. And God has continued to love us and forgive us, though we are no different than the Israelites.

As Moses went continually to God, on behalf of Israel, he learned patience, peace, love, kindness, goodness, faithfulness, and self control. In other words, Moses learned the fruits of the Spirit. By being with God he learned God's ways. He has to have learned forgiveness too, because he was taking the same sins from the same people to God, asking forgiveness over and over again for them.

There again, Jesus does the same for us. He goes before God on our behalf, asking forgiveness for us. Does that mean we do not need to pray, that Jesus is doing it for us? Absolutely not! We need to go to Jesus, our Advocate, so He will take our petitions to God.

If we linger in God's Presence, we will see God's Glory and Love. Moses talked to God and was with God and had asked God to show him His Glory. God had told him He would walk in front of him, and that He would proclaim His name. He said no man could see His face and live. The Lord said, "Here is a place by Me, and you shall stand on the rock. So it shall be, while My glory passes by, that I will put you in a cleft of the rock, and will cover you with My hand, while I pass by. Then I will take away My hand and you shall see My back; but My face shall not be seen." Exodus 33:21-23

Moses was with God several times and had seen His Glory. Like Moses, the more we are with God, the more we want to be with Him, and the more we want to be like Him. Each time Moses was with God he fell more and more in love with Him, as we do when we spend time with Him.

The Lord asked Moses to chisel out two more stones and bring them to Him so He could write the Ten Commandments again.

So Moses did this and took them up on Mt. Sinai. The Lord came down in a cloud and stood with him and proclaimed His name. Moses bowed down to the ground and worshiped Him. The Lord told Moses He was making a covenant with him and with Israel, to do wonders never done before in any nation in the world.

When Moses came down from the mountain, his face was radiant because he had been with God. The Israelites could see the Glory of the Lord or the light or "Heavenly Bliss" on Moses' face. God's Shekinah Glory was with Moses. Shekinah is Hebrew meaning "to dwell." Moses had dwelt with God, and His Light shone on Moses' face.

God had given Moses specific instructions to build a Tabernacle, where He could dwell with His people. The Tabernacle was to be a portable Temple revealed to Moses by God, where the people could come and commune with God. They could only come through blood atonement, with a priest as their mediator.

God said, "Let them make Me a sanctuary that I may dwell among them." Exodus 25:8-9

The Tabernacle was the focal point for the camp of Israel, with three tribes of Israel camped on each of the four sides. God's Shekinah Glory dwelt in the Holy of Holies of the Tabernacle, and the Commandments and Law were to direct all the people to God.

The Tabernacle was to be in the shape of a rectangle and was to be divided into two sections which were (1.) the Holy Place and (2.) the Most Holy Place, (also called the Holy of Holies.) It was to be covered by goat hair, as a tent, over the Tabernacle, with ram skins dyed red, and a covering of badger skins above that, making a triple layer, as a protective covering for the Tabernacle and all the articles for worship inside. (Exodus 26:7&14)

The first covering, the goat hair curtain, symbolized the Law of Moses, sending the goat to the wilderness bearing the sin of the people and was a symbol of Jesus Christ bearing the sin of mankind as He hung on the cross.

The ram skins and the badger skins were a covering of protection over the goat hair for the Tabernacle. Their outside covering was nothing to look at, but there was a pretty color underneath. Jesus had no beauty that we should desire Him. (Isaiah 53:2) But He had all the love and a heart of gold on the inside.

The Court of the Tabernacle, or the outer court, held the Tabernacle and all its furnishings. The Court of the Tabernacle completely surrounded the area where the sacrifices were made, the Holy Place and the Holy of Holies.

The entrance gate to the Court of the Tabernacle was made with curtains made of blue, purple, and scarlet thread, and fine woven linen. (Exodus 27:16) The blue thread was symbolic of heaven, purity and obedience. Blue was also associated with the commandments of God, the importance of remembering them, and the heavenly calling of those who had been chosen by God to be His people. The robe of the High Priest was also blue, representing the close association with God and His word.

The color purple represented royalty and status. As they took Jesus to crucify Him, they put a purple robe on Him.

"And they clothed Him with purple; and they twisted a crown of thorns, put it on His head, and began to salute Him, " Hail, King of the Jews!" Mark 15:17-18

Scarlet is associated with sin.

"Though your sins are like scarlet, they shall be as white as snow." Isaiah 1:18

The fine woven linen was of the best quality and was worn by the priests and also was worn by Jesus after He died on the cross.

"So Joseph bought fine linen cloth, took Him down, and wrapped Him in the linen. And he laid Him in a tomb which had been hewn out of the rock, and rolled a stone against the door of the tomb." Mark 15:46

Looking all the way back to the farthest end of the Court of the Tabernacle, we could see a portable building housing the Holy Place and the Most Holy Place or Holy of Holies. Standing in the Holy of Holies, we could see the Ark of the Covenant. The Ark of the Covenant was made of acacia wood and overlaid with pure gold. Moses and the High Priest (Aaron) were the only two who could enter into the Most Holy Place or Holy of Holies, where the Ark of the Covenant was placed. (Exodus 25:10-11) The Ark of the Covenant was covered with a blue cloth representing its close association with the Word of God. The two tablets of stone with the Ten Commandments, which was Israel's law, were in the Ark of the Covenant.

Also, in the Holy of Holies was the Mercy Seat. The Mercy Seat was of pure gold, and it held two cherubim (Angels) hammered out, one on each of the two ends of the mercy seat. The cherubim stretched out their wings above, covering the Mercy Seat with their wings. The faces of the cherubim were toward the Mercy Seat, facing one another. The Mercy Seat was on top of the Ark of the Covenant in the Holy of Holies. The Ark of the Covenant was the only piece of furniture in the Holy of Holies. The High Priest came and communed with God above the Mercy Seat on behalf of the Israelites, in the Holy of Holies, once a year. God's Glory was between the two cherubim on the mercy seat. The Glory of the Lord was the light in the Holy of Holies. (Exodus 25:17-22)

In the Holy Place, we could find the <u>Table for the Showbread</u>. It was overlaid with gold and had a frame of gold around it. The dishes, pans, pitchers, and bowls that were set on the Showbread Table were also made of pure gold. There were twelve loaves of bread placed on the showbread table, six in a row, and one for each of the twelve tribes of Israel. Fresh bread replaced the old bread each Sabbath. The table for the showbread was placed on the north side of the Holy Place.

The Showbread Table signified the union of Jesus' divine and human nature. His divine and human nature were united together in one Person here on earth. (Exodus 25:23-30)

The Golden Lampstand or Candlestick was also in the Holy Place, on the south side across from the Showbread Table. It was a hammered work of pure gold with a central shaft and six branches, three on either side. Each stem had an almond-blossom-shaped bowl to hold pure olive oil, and an ornamental knob and a flower. The Lampstand was to burn continually, and part of the priests' ministry was to keep the lamp burning. The lampstand was to provide light as God is the Light of the world.

The Altar of Incense stood in the Holy Place, right in front of the veiled Holy of Holies. The Altar was to burn incense and was made of acacia wood. Aaron, the High Priest, burned incense every morning and evening. The incense was to be made of sweet spices of stacte, onycha, galbanum, and pure frankincense. The stacte was a sweet gum exuded from the Storax tree (similar to a Poplar tree) growing in Israel. The onycha came from the shells of the mollusk. When it was burned, it gave off a perfumed fragrance. Galbanum was a gum resin that emitted a milky sap with a balsamic odor. Frankincense was a fragrant white gum that came from the Salai Tree in Arabia. The smoke from the incense curled upward, representing the prayers of God's people.

The Veil (meaning to separate) was a curtain between the Holy Place and the Most Holy Place. It was woven from fine woven linen, of blue, purple and scarlet thread. The blue, purple and scarlet were the colors of royalty. The fine linen was to represent the purity of Christ. The veil was a barrier between God and man. It was designed with Cherubim on it and was hung upon the four pillars of acacia wood overlaid with gold. Jesus changed the veil from a barrier to a gateway with the cross of Calvary. When Jesus died on the cross, the veil split in two, signifying that we can go to God without an animal sacrifice. Jesus was the Sacrifice, also signifying the Holy of Holies could be entered without fear by all believers/priests.

The Brazen Laver was in the outer court of the Tabernacle. It had no measurements and was used only by the priest for purification. The priest would wash his right hand and foot and then his left hand and foot. This ritual was done each time the priest entered the outer court.

The Brazen Altar was an open box made of acacia wood overlaid with brass with a horn on each of the four corners. The wood represented the "Works of the Flesh"

"If anyone builds on this foundation with gold, silver, wood, hay, straw, each one's work will become clear; for the Day will declare it, because it will be revealed by fire; and the fire will test each one's work, of what sort it is." I Corinthians 3:12-13

If the wood was directly exposed to the fire, it would be reduced to ashes. The Brass was the shield for the wood, as God is our shield. Because of the combination of the wood and the brass, men can declare:

"I can do all things through Christ who strengthens me." Philippians 4:13

The blood-stained horns pointed upward and outward to the four corners of the world, reminding us that God is in all four corners of the earth and reminding us of the power of Christ's blood that will be witnessed throughout the world. It also reminds us of God's Great Commission to us to proclaim the gospel throughout the world. The Brazen Altar was in the outer court of the Tabernacle, and the position of the altar was open to the Israelites, so they could atone for their sins.

The Brazen Altar and the Cross of Christ both spoke of justification. Israel was restored to a right relationship with God by offering a blood sacrifice. We are restored through the sacrifice of Jesus' blood on the cross and justified through the Grace of God.

"The law was given through Moses, but grace and truth came through Jesus Christ." John 1:17

After the Tabernacle was erected, the Israelites would bring their sacrifices to the priest, who offered them as a burnt offering for the sins of the people. Jesus was the sacrificial Lamb for our sins, and we should bring them to the foot of the cross daily.

The Tabernacle was a picture to show the Israelites how to worship by God's design. Why is the Tabernacle important today? God's Presence was in the Holy of Holies. His presence, the Holy Spirit, now dwells in us, His children. The Brazen Altar was for Israel's sin sacrifice. Christ is our sin sacrifice. The Laver was for the cleansing of the priest. We are cleansed through our confession of sin to God through His Son, Jesus Christ. The Lampstand was a light in the Holy Place. We (God's Children) are enlightened by the Holy Spirit, and then we serve as a light to the world. The Table for the Showbread was a continual reminder of God's promise to Israel of the covenant between God and Israel and was a memorial of God's provision for Israel. We are fed by the living word. The Altar of Incense represented the prayers of the faithful. We can pray and have intercession and communication daily with God. The Veil separated God and man. Now through Jesus, we can enter God's Presence, boldly, through Christ. Jesus Christ is our gateway to God!

God instructed Moses concerning the rituals of the Tabernacle, reminding Israel of the covenant with Him. God's Glory hovered over the cherubim in the Holy of Holies and the people saw God's Glory over the mountain and they saw God's glory on Moses' face when he came down from the mountain.

God's Glory is a part of His realm. It is the realm of eternity. It is the revelation of the Presence of God. It is the manifestation of His Presence. He is Glory. He is everywhere, and Glory is the manifestation of that reality. Earth has the atmosphere of air, whereas the heavenly atmosphere is Glory, His Presence. When Glory comes down, it is a bit of heaven's atmosphere coming down to us, a taste of His Manifest Presence.

Some people don't want to believe unless they can see. But, we don't see the air, do we? All of us would be dead, if we were not breathing the air that we cannot see. We are not conscious of the air, unless we see the wind blowing the leaves on the trees. Yet, the earth is covered by it. In the same way, not one inch of Heaven lacks Glory. Now, God is giving us a taste of that Glory, Heaven manifested on earth.[2]

Even though God had given Israel the Tabernacle, and He wanted to be their one true God, Israel had fallen back into sin and worshiped false idols, grumbling and complaining about all that God had provided

"I am the First and I am the Last; Besides Me there is no God." Isaiah 44:6

When we obey God, He will manifest His Glory and favor to His children. We experience His Glory by worshiping Him and coming into His Presence, through spending time in prayer. We need to linger in prayer with God and worship Him and sing praises to Him. The longer we stay in prayer with God, the more we will experience Him and know Him.

We, as God's Children, have God's Presence dwelling within us through the Holy Spirit. As we pray and seek His face, we should ask God to show us His Glory! We should never settle for less than His Glory.

Praise and Glory to God on the highest!

GLORIOUS SAVIOR

Glorious morning, sent from above
Jesus, my Savior, sends down His love
Faithful He is, true to His word
Majestic Councilor, as no one has heard
Worshiped with gladness, praising His name
Honor and Glory, without any shame
Love and acceptance, placing no blame
Worthy, so worthy, is the Lamb that was slain

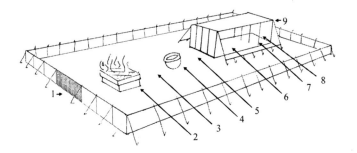

DIMENSIONS FOR TABERNACLE

1. Outer Gate – 30 feet wide
2. Brazen Altar in outer court – 71/2 feet long x 71/2 feet wide x 41/2feet high
3. Court Yard – 30 feet long x 71/2 feet wide
4. Brazen Laver – No Dimensions
5. Tabernacle – 36 inches long x 18 inches wide x 15 feet high
6. The Holy Place – 30 feet long x 15 feet wide
7. The Veil – The curtain between the Holy Place and the Most Holy Place
8. Most Holy Place or Holy of Holies – 15 feet square
9. Court of Tabernacle – 150 feet long x 75 feet wide

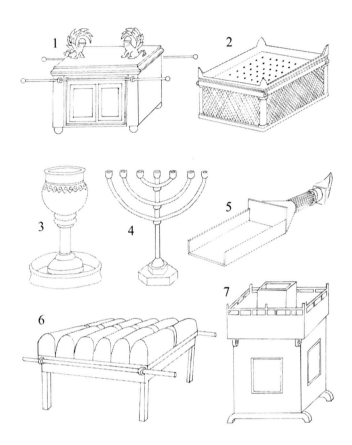

DIMENSIONS FOR ARTICLES OF TABERNACLE

1. Ark of Covenant with the Mercy Seat - 45 inches long x 27 inches wide x 27 inches high
2. Brazen Altar – 7 ½ feet long x 7 ½ feet wide x 4 ½ feet high
3. Laver used in Holy Place – No Dimensions
4. Lampstand or Candlestick – No Dimensions
5. Incense Holder - No Dimensions
6. Showbread Table – 36 inches long x 15 feet wide x 27 inches high
7. Altar of Incense – 1 ½ feet long x 1 ½ feet wide x 3 feet

6

ON HOLY GROUND

The Tabernacle was now ready for worship. The Israelites were to bring an offering to the Lord from their herds, flocks, and birds. The sacrifice had to be the best of the best and brought as a free-will offering.

The Tabernacle was the place of sacrificial worship, and the Israelites had to atone for their sins. They had already entered into the covenant relationship with God. This covenant was a binding relationship and was a concept of grace and law. The Israelites were to follow God in obedience and faith.

The blood sacrifices or offerings were of great significance and were the perfect atonement for sin. The sacrifices taught the Israelites how to worship through personal commitment.

There were five different offerings made by the priest and the Israelites in their covenant with God.

There were three sweet-savor offerings and two non-sweet-savor offerings. The sweet-savor offerings demonstrated that Christ was acceptable to God. The non-sweet-savor offering demonstrated that the sinner was unacceptable, but that God's justice fell upon Christ, as He became the sinner's Substitute.

(1.) <u>The Burnt Offering</u> was offered at the door of the Tabernacle. The type of animal offered was a male without blemish and was brought according to what each Israelite could afford. The rich people brought a bull or an ox; the middle class people brought a sheep or a goat; and the poor people brought turtle doves or pigeons. Each person was to bring according to his prosperity. This offering was made by fire, which is a sweet-savor-offering unto the Lord and typified Christ as the perfect Sacrifice on our behalf. The person bringing the offering was to bring it before the Lord and the priests. Aaron's sons were to build a fire upon the altar and bring the blood of the burnt offering and sprinkle it all around the altar. They had to skin the animal and cut it into pieces. They were to wash the legs and entrails with water. And all of it was to be burned on the altar as a sacrifice, signifying their complete and total surrender to God. This also typifies the will of Jesus, as He voluntarily offered Himself on the cross.

The Israelites were to kill the animal on the north side of the altar. As they drew the knife across the animal's throat, they would remember the ugliness of their sin. Each time they saw a bull, ox, sheep, goat, pigeon, or turtle dove, they were reminded.

The offering of the fowl for the burnt offering was handled differently. The one bringing the offering was not to handle the bird. That was the priests' job. The birds were killed by wringing their necks, and the blood was offered at the side of the altar for the atonement. The bird was cut down the middle, and the insides were removed. The burnt offering was offered daily by the priest to remind the Israelites to consecrate themselves to God. But the priest had to atone for their own sins before they could bring the sacrifice to God for the Israelites.

"Then you shall set the altar of the burnt offering before the door of the tabernacle of the tent of meeting." Exodus 40:6

Just as the Israelites were reminded of their sin through the sacrifices, we are reminded of the price Christ paid for us, through the reading of God's Word, taking communion, or going to church and hearing God's Word proclaimed.

(2.) The Grain or Meal Offering was a sweet-savor-offering and pictured the perfect Person and character of Christ. The desire to know more about Christ was the depiction of the meal offering. It consisted of an offering of fine flour, frankincense and oil stirred together with no lumps, as Jesus displayed no unevenness in His humanity. The oil was used as a symbol of the Holy Spirit and mixed with the finely ground flour, giving off a pleasing aroma when the fire was applied. It was to be brought before the priest as a memorial on the altar. Salt was also used in the meal offering to preserve the meal, to arrest corruption and to depict God's covenant relationship between Israel and God. A "Covenant of Salt" was used in the sacrificial meal that accompanied the making of the covenant between Israel and God, as we are to be the "Salt of the Earth.

"You are the salt of the earth." Matthew 5:13

Any green grain that was used was dried over the fire and beaten to remove the husk and then used as a grain or meal offering. Jesus pictured Himself as a grain of wheat that had to die to produce fruit.

"Unless a grain of wheat falls into the ground and dies, it remains alone; but if it dies, it produces much grain." John 12:24

Through Jesus' death on the cross, He brought resurrection life to all who put their faith in Him.

(3.) <u>The Peace Offering</u> was a sweet-savor offering, and the animal could be a male or female without blemish. The peace offering was shared by the Israelites and the priests' before God. The peace offering was made by fire because it took judgment to bring peace. God's portion was burned on the altar, which speaks of communion and fellowship. The priests and the one presenting the peace offering were asking for the peace and fellowship of God. The one bringing the offering was to put his hand upon its head and kill the animal at the door of the Tabernacle. The priest was to take the blood and sprinkle it all around on the altar. The breast and right shoulder was waved before God. The breast symbolized love and affection, and the shoulder symbolized strength. The animal fat, the tail, the two kidneys and liver were removed and burned on the altar as food, to make an offering made by fire unto the Lord.

Once the offering was made and reconciliation was accomplished by sprinkling of the blood, the priest was to eat of the sacrifice. Shalom, in Hebrew, means peace, and Jesus Christ is our perfect Peace. God's thoughts toward His people are peaceful. Believers can experience His peace by asking for peace in faith and obedience. The priest prayed for the peace of the Israelites, and at Jesus' birth, the angels proclaimed peace. Peace is talked about all through the Bible, and God is a God of Peace and the Prince of Peace.

"And the peace of God, which surpasses all understanding, will guard your hearts and minds through Christ Jesus." Philippians 4:7

(4.) <u>The Sin Offering</u> was not a sweet-savor-offering. The sin offering dealt with the root of the sin, and the guilt of the sin was taken away. Restoration was brought in its place. The Sin Offering stood in contrast to the Burnt Offering. The Burnt Offering was all for God, while the Sin Offering was all for man. In the Burnt Offering, the believer is seen as identified with Christ. In the Sin Offering, Christ is seen as identified with the believer's sin. The sacrifice had to be without blemish. Christ, as our sacrificial Lamb, was without spot or blemish. The sin offering was killed at the door of the Tabernacle by the one bringing the offering. Then the priest dipped his finger into the blood and sprinkled it seven times before the Lord, in front of the veil of the sanctuary. The blood sprinkled in front of the veil signified the shedding of Christ's blood. Then the priest put some of the blood on the horns of the altar of incense before the Lord, and the remaining blood was poured at the base of the altar of the burnt offering. Then the priests would remove all the fat, the fat on the entrails, and the fat on the flanks, the fat on the two kidneys, and the fat on the liver. Then the sacrifice was burned on the altar of burnt offerings. The hide, flesh, head, legs, entrails (intestines) and offal (internal organs) were taken outside the camp and burned to ashes, as Christ died outside the city walls of Jerusalem.

"Therefore, Jesus also, that He might sanctify the people with His own blood, suffered outside the gate." Hebrews 13:12

With the sin offering, the blood was within the veil, indicating the sacrifice had been acceptable. Then, the ashes were spread outside the camp. Christ, outside the camp, died for us. Christ, inside the veil, is living for us and standing at the right hand of God and interceding on our behalf.

(5.) The Trespass offering was a non-sweet-savor-offering. The Trespass Offering dealt with the conviction of sin and expiation (the penalty for sin) and involved restitution. The guilt and conviction of sin was taken away, and the one presenting the offering was restored. The cleansing of sin was made through the confession of the sin.

God wants His people to be a holy people. He wanted that for Israel, and He wants that for us. He wants every area of our lives to be in order and placed under His Lordship. He wants our every word and every thought to be under His care and for us to honor Him. He wants us to come to Him daily and to consecrate ourselves daily to Him.

"Consecrate yourselves, therefore, and be holy, for I am the Lord your God." Leviticus 20:7

God gave His directions for holy living and emphasized the importance of living within His commands. He explained fully how to bring a sacrifice that was pleasing to Him. God has the perfect moral nature and wanted to teach Israel how to live for Him.

God spoke to Moses, telling him to bring Aaron and his sons, who were the priests, the priests clothing, the anointing oil, a bull as a sin offering, two rams, and a basket of unleavened bread and to gather the congregation at the door of the Tabernacle.

Moses did as the Lord commanded him. These were the first sacrifices made to the Lord after the Tabernacle was built. The congregation gathered at the door of the Tabernacle and Moses said to them,

"This is what the Lord commanded to be done." Leviticus 8:5

Aaron and his sons were there, and Moses washed the priests with water. Moses put the High Priests clothing on Aaron, which consisted of the tunic, the robe, the ephod and the breastplate. He put the Urim and the Thummim (the lights and perfections) in the breastplate, which was over the heart. The breastplate was square and was made of gold, blue, purple and scarlet yarn and finely twisted linen. The breastplate was set with three rows of four stones. There was a colored stone for each tribe of Israel on the breastplate. The first row of stones consisted of the sardius, topaz and emerald. The second row of stones consisted of the turquoise, sapphire and diamond. The third row of stones consisted of the jacinth, agate and amethyst. The fourth row of stones consisted of the beryl, onyx and jasper. Each stone was engraved with one name of each tribe of Israel. Two gold chains with two gold rings were holding the breastplate in place over the ephod. The gold chains were connected at the seam of the ephod under the shoulder straps.

The robe was made of blue fine woven linen with bells and pomegranates sewn along the bottom. The bells were of pure gold and the pomegranates were made of blue, purple, and scarlet threads. There was a bell between each pomegranate.

Moses put the turban on Aaron's head. On the front of it, he added the golden plate and put the holy crown upon his head. The golden plate was made of pure gold and was fastened to the turban with a blue cord. The words "HOLINESS TO THE LORD" were inscribed on the plate.

Moses took the anointing oil and anointed the Tabernacle and all that was in it. He sprinkled some of the oil on the altar seven times, anointing the altar and all its utensils. Also, he anointed the laver and its base. He then poured some of the oil on Aaron's head and anointed him to consecrate him.

Then Moses brought Aaron's sons and put tunics on them, girding them with sashes, and put turbans on them, as the Lord had commanded.

Next, Moses brought the bull for the sin offering. Aaron and his sons laid their hands on the head of the bull, and Moses killed it. Next, Moses took some of the blood and sprinkled it all around on the horns of the altar and purified the altar. He then poured the blood at the base of the altar, consecrating it, to make atonement for it. He then took all the fat and the fat tail; the fatty lobe attached to the liver, and the two kidneys and their fat and burned them on the altar. But the bull, its hide, its flesh and its offal, he burned outside the camp, as the Lord had commanded.

Then he brought the ram, as the burnt offering. The burnt offering followed the sin offering because it was impossible to comprehend the value of Christ until sin was dealt with in a manner pleasing to God. The sin offering represented what Christ did for us on the cross and the burnt offering dealt with who Christ is to us.

Aaron and his sons laid their hands on the head of the ram, and Moses killed it. Next, he sprinkled the blood all around on the altar and cut the ram into pieces, and Moses burned the head, the pieces and the fat. Next, he washed the entrails and the legs in water. Then, he burned the whole ram on the altar. It was a burnt offering for a sweet aroma to the Lord, an offering made by fire, as the Lord had commanded.

Then Moses brought the second ram, as the ram of consecration. The ram of consecration was a trespass offering unto the Lord because the priests were already in the sanctuary. Aaron and his sons laid their hands on the head of the ram, and Moses killed it. Moses took some of the blood and put it on the tip of Aaron's right ear and on the thumb of his right hand and on the big toe of his right foot. Then he brought Aaron's sons and put some of the blood on the tips of their right ears, on the thumb of their right hands, and on the big toe of their right feet.

The blood on the tip of the priests' ear symbolized the priest would hear the voice of God. The blood-tipped thumb was essential for service of God. And the blood-tipped foot was essential for the walk before the Lord. This is all symbolic of the fact that the whole person must be presented before the Lord.

Moses sprinkled the blood all around on the altar. Then he took the fat, the fat tail, the fat on the liver, two kidneys and right thigh; from the basket of unleavened bread, he took a cake of bread anointed with oil, and one wafer. Then he put them on the fat and on the right thigh. And he put all these in Aaron's hands and his sons' hands and waved them as a wave offering before the Lord.

The wave offering was a consistent repeated horizontal motion signifying the Lord was the Ruler of the earth. The wave offering signified a total commitment to God made by the one offering.

Then Moses took them from their hands and burned them on the altar on the burnt offering. They were consecration offerings for a sweet aroma and that was an offering made by fire before the Lord. And Moses took the breast and waved it as a wave offering. It was Moses' part of the ram of consecration, as the Lord had commanded Moses.

Then Moses took some of the anointing oil and some of the blood which was on the altar and sprinkled it on Aaron, his garments, his sons and their garments, and he consecrated Aaron, his sons and their garments. (Leviticus 8:6-13)

Moses said to Aaron and his sons,

"Boil the flesh at the door of the tabernacle of meeting, and eat it there with the bread that is in the basket of consecration offering." Leviticus 8:31

Aaron and his sons did as Moses commanded, and the remains were burned with fire. Then Moses told them not to go out the door of the Tabernacle for seven days, until the day of their consecration had ended. So, for seven days and nights, they stood in the door of the Tabernacle to keep watch for the Lord. If they had disobeyed Moses, they would have died. But Aaron and his sons did as they were commanded by Moses.

After seven days, Moses came to Aaron and his sons and commanded them to take a bull as a sin offering and a ram as a burnt offering. And to the children of Israel, he told them to take a kid of the goats and make a sin offering and a calf and a lamb as a burnt offering, and a bull and a ram as a peace offering, and to sacrifice before the Lord a grain offering mixed with oil, and Moses said,

"And the glory of the Lord will appear to you." Leviticus 9:6

So they brought all the animals that Moses had commanded them before the Tabernacle, and Aaron went to the altar and killed the calf for the sin offering. And the sons of Aaron brought the blood to him, and they went through the same ritual as Moses had done seven days before.

They brought all the offerings before the Lord, as had been done before, and then Aaron lifted his hand toward the people, blessing them as he and Moses completed the sin offering, burnt offering, and peace offering.

Then the glory of the Lord appeared to all the people and fire came before the Lord and consumed the burnt offering and the fat on the altar. When all the people saw what the Lord had done, they shouted and fell on their faces.

Then Nadab and Abihu, the sons of Aaron, each took a censor and put fire in it and put incense on it and offered it before the Lord, which He had not commanded them to do. So fire went out from the Lord and devoured them, and they died before the Lord.

God wanted obedience from His people. He would tolerate nothing less. This act of God may seem a bit too harsh to us, but Nadab and Abihu were being disrespectful and disobedient.

The Lord spoke to Moses after the death of Aaron's two sons, saying:

"Tell Aaron, your brother, not to come at just any time into the Holy Place inside the veil, before the mercy seat which is on the Ark, lest he die; for I will appear in the cloud above the mercy seat. Thus, Aaron shall come into the Holy Place: with the blood of the young bull as a sin offering, and of a ram as a burnt offering." Leviticus 16:2-3

At the correct time, as the Lord had spoken, He appeared in the cloud above the Mercy Seat. This was the Day of Atonement, when the people would atone for their sins through the Priest, and the one day of the year that Aaron was to come into the Most Holy Place or the Holy of Holies with the blood of a young bull as a sin offering and a ram as a burnt offering for himself and his family. Aaron washed his body and put on the holy linen tunic and trousers and the linen sash and turban to make the sacrifices. The children of Israel were to bring two kid goats as a sin offering and one ram as a burnt offering.

Aaron was to take the bull and make a sin offering for himself and his household. Then he took the two goats that were given by the children of Israel, and presented them before the Lord at the door of the Tabernacle. Aaron cast lots for the two goats: one lot was for the Lord, and the other lot was for the scapegoat. The goat that was the Lord's was to be given as the Sin Offering. The other goat was to be presented alive before the Lord, to make atonement for it. Then, it was to be released into the wilderness as the scapegoat.

Aaron was to kill the bull for the sin offering, which was to be made for himself and for his household. Then he was to take a censer full of burning coals of fire from the altar before the Lord; with his hands full of incense, he was to take it inside the veil into the Most Holy Place (Holy of Holies). He was to put the incense on the fire before the Lord. The cloud of incense would cover the Mercy Seat, which was on the Ark of the Covenant. He took some of the blood of the bull and sprinkled it with his finger on the mercy seat on the east side, and then he sprinkled some of the blood with this finger seven times on the mercy seat.

Next, he took some of the blood of the bull and sprinkled it on the horns of the altar all around. He then sprinkled some of the blood on his finger seven times, asking God to cleanse and consecrate him and his family from all uncleanness. Everything had to be as God directed.

Then Aaron killed the goat for the sins of the people. This sin offering was to be sprinkled on the mercy seat in the same manner as the offering Aaron had used for himself and his family. Again, Aaron went to the altar and sprinkled the blood of the sacrifice for the sins of the people. He did exactly as he had done for his own sacrifice. He sprinkled the blood on the horns of the altar for the sins of the people, asking God to forgive them and cleanse them and consecrate them from all uncleanness.

When he had atoned for their sins, he brought in the live goat. He laid both hands on the head of the goat and confessed over it all the iniquities of the people. The goat was to bear all the sins for the people. He then released the goat, and it was taken by another member of the Israelites into the wilderness.

Then Aaron came into the Tabernacle, taking off his priestly clothing, which he had put on to go into the Most Holy Place. He washed his body with water in the Holy Place, put on his garments, and then came out and offered his burnt offering and the burnt offering of the people, to make atonement for himself and for the people. The bull and the goat that were used as the sin offering were taken outside the camp. Each one was burned by a member of the tribe of Israel. Then, that person washed himself and came back into the camp.

Once a year, the priest would pass through the great veil or curtain and enter the Holy of Holies, ready to bring the blood of the sacrifice upon the altar for the sins of the people.

The Israelites were standing outside the Tabernacle, waiting to see if the priest would reappear, hoping against hope that God would accept the sacrifice brought to Him by the priest. If the priest didn't reappear, that meant that God had not accepted the sacrifice and Israel's sins were not forgiven. If this happened the priest was put to death by God. The priest had a cord tied around his ankle, so others could drag him out of the Most Holy Place if God did not accept the sacrifice, because no one could enter the Most Holy Place but the most High Priest.

The great curtain or veil which stood between God and the people was a constant reminder of the great gulf of sin between them. God could have left it that way. He could have never forgiven them of their sin. But He loved them too much. He had built the bridge for them to cross, through the sin sacrifice. He could have turned His back on Israel because of His fury with them, but He had not. He just wanted to show them His love and wanted their obedience so He could pour out His blessings upon them.

"For the life of the flesh is in the blood, and I have given it to you upon the altar to make atonement for your souls; for it is the blood that makes atonement for the soul." Leviticus 17:11

For Israel, worship was centered on the altar. The altar of sacrifice was the focal point of the Tabernacle to provide a place where the people could approach God.

They could bring their sacrifices daily for the burnt offering. Think of what the priests and the Israelites had gone through. Can you imagine the smell of all the animals, of all the blood and the slaughter?

Think of all the noise of millions of people and the noise of all the animals. Think of what the priests' clothing must have looked like by the end of the day. Even though the Israelites could come daily and bring a burnt offering, this was not an easy task for anyone. The animals had no power to atone for sin. They were used as a substitute for the life of the one offering the sacrifice. The sacrifice was the basis of the approach to God, and God demanded a clean people. God wanted a people who wanted to be righteous and would come to Him for a daily cleansing. The animal sacrifice pointed to the great sacrifice that would be made by our Savior. After Jesus (the perfect Lamb) was slain, there was no need for another sacrifice.

For us, the day of sacrifice is over. The Sacrifice has been paid once for all!

Now you may want to ask, what does this have to do with me and my walk with God? Everything that was done in the Tabernacle in the Old Testament was a preview of what would happen in the New Testament. For example, the priests interceded for the people, before God, when they offered the sacrifice. Jesus interceded in the New Testament for all mankind. And, He called us to be priests and intercede for others.

So, having some understanding of the Old Testament lays a foundation for more fully understanding the New Testament.

Prayer is the tool we use to intercede for others. Intercession has always been costly. In the Old Testament, bringing the animals cost the people. Jesus paid the ultimate price to intercede for us-His own life.

But are we willing to pay the price to intercede for others, sacrificing time, sleep, giving up our will for God's will? We need to consider the cost, personally, before we answer!

Can we rejoice in knowing God through prayer? Yes, by all means! When we have difficulties in life, if we will continue to look to God for the answers to our problems, keep our eyes focused on Him, and continue to pray, He will answer. He can and will do far more than we could ever imagine. We can always believe that God will answer and always wants what is best for His children. I have found that if I stay in the center of God's will for my life, He will bless me far beyond my imagination. There is definitely power in prayer, because God is waiting to answer our prayers. God can even give us the foreknowledge of prayer, which means we can believe that something is going to happen before it actually does happen. We can believe this through the Holy Spirit, who dwells within us. There is wisdom in prayer, and God gives all His children wisdom, if we ask. We can rejoice in knowing that God will and does answer our prayers.

You may ask, "Why is life so difficult, even if we pray?" or "What would life be like without prayer? God said that we would have many trials and tribulations, but that He had overcome the world. We are to grow through our tribulations. God never leaves us the same. When He comes into our life, He is there to slowly change us, making us into what He wants us to become, which is more like Him. When a child of God has wronged us, we need to remember that they are still learning, even as we are. So we need to forego harshness and have a forgiving spirit.

"Count it all joy when you fall into various trials, knowing that the testing of your faith produces patience." James 1:2-3

God wants us to persevere. Sometimes it is hard to keep on keeping on, but if we will continue to pray and seek God's will, He will answer our prayers and show us the path He wants us to seek. This is where we need our faith.

Without prayer, I shudder to think what life would be like. What would our children grow up to be if we never disciplined them or told them anything to do? Can you imagine life without love, guidance, or safety? Life without prayer would be like this earth without God. Satan could and would take over to a greater extent, and it would be a life without hope or love. We would be destitute.

God gives us wisdom in prayer and through His Holy Spirit who is residing within us, His children.

Going to God in prayer should start with praise. Next, we should ask for forgiveness of our sins. Reflect over the day or the previous day, naming our sins, one by one, as we remember each one of them. God knows our sins, but He wants us to recognize them. The more we recognize the same sin, the more we can consciously try not to commit that sin. We need to thank God for all He has done on our behalf and then intercede for others, bringing their needs before God. And then, we need to commit our lives and hearts to God daily. All of this may sound like a chore. It is not. If we will commit to God, He will guide us and show us how to pray and what he wants us to do.

It will come naturally and easily. We can come to God day or night. Speak to Him as to your best Friend, because He is.

It might be helpful to look over the following types of prayer and the explanation for each.
There are seven types of prayer:

1. <u>Prayer of Agreement</u> - is being in agreement with God while praying His Word. And it also involves being in agreement with others with whom you are praying.

2. <u>Secret (Closet) Prayers</u> - going into your Prayer Closet, talking to God alone, and telling Him the desires of your heart.

3. <u>Prayer of Petition</u> – is asking God for His help. And with God's grace, He will help us.

4. <u>Prayer of Thanksgiving</u> - is being thankful for what He has already given us. More praise and thanking God brings more answers to prayers.

5. <u>Prayer of Intercession</u> - is coming to God on behalf of others.

6. <u>Prayer of Commitment</u> – is putting the situation or person in God's hands.

7. <u>Prayer of Consecration</u> – is giving our actions or our lives to God, daily, asking God to separate us from the world's way of thinking.

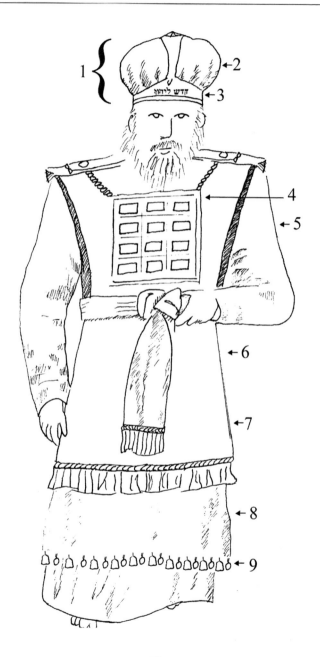

PRIEST CLOTHING

1. Holy Crown
2. Turban
3. Golden Plate
4. Breastplate
5. Tunic
6. Sash
7. Ephod
8. Robe
9. Bells and Pomegranates

7

A HOLY CONVOCATION

(A holy meeting)

God wanted Israel to focus on their relationship with Him by celebrating and remembering where they had been. He wanted them to remember that He had taken them out of their bondage from Egypt, and He would take them to the Promised Land. God wanted them to worship and to thank Him for what He had done for them. Through the religious celebrations, God wanted them to realize the spiritual road map for living and to stay in tune with God.

And the Lord spoke to Moses, saying, "Speak to the children of Israel, and say to them: The feasts of the Lord, which you shall proclaim to be holy convocations, these are My feasts." Leviticus 23:1-2

The Lord asked the children of Israel to work for six days and then to have a "<u>Shabbat</u>," a day of rest. "<u>Shabbat</u>" is Hebrew for Sabbath.

The <u>Sabbath or Shabbat</u> was twenty-five hours long and began on Friday afternoon, eighteen minutes before sunset and went through Saturday night, after the stars came out. The start of the Sabbath changed each week because of the change of the sunset.

The Sabbath began with the lighting of two candles. Two candles were used because the Ten Commandments were mentioned twice in the Hebrew scripture.

<u>The first mention</u> at Mount Sinai was:

"Remember the Sabbath day and keep it holy." Exodus 20:8

<u>The second mention</u> at Mount Sinai was: "Observe the Sabbath day to keep it holy, as the Lord your God commanded you." Deuteronomy 5:12

The primary goal of the Sabbath was to focus on the spiritual renewal of Israel's faith. God wanted Israel to remember the Sabbath and observe it as a holy day each week. He gave the example and showed the importance of this day of rest after creating Adam and Eve in Genesis 2:1-2. He even included the animals and the land in this day of rest as indicated in Exodus 23:12.

A short prayer marked the Sabbath as being sacred and special and was followed by a Kiddush (Holy) Prayer with wine or grape juice. This was a prayer to sanctify the day, bless the children and the spouse, celebrate with a festive meal, and singing. This was finished with a prayer of thanksgiving after the meal. This basic ritual was repeated at the lunch on the Sabbath and the late evening meal. After the late evening meal on the Sabbath, there was worship and study of the Torah. The Sabbath concluded with a ritual called Havdalah (a brief ceremony that marked the transition between the Sabbath and the rest of the week.)

"Consecrate yourselves therefore, and be holy, for I am the Lord your God. And you shall keep My statutes, and perform them: I am the Lord who sanctifies you." Leviticus 20:7-8

The Lord wanted Israel to worship on the Sabbath and make it a day of rest, but He also wanted Israel to have a Holy Convocation with Feasts.

"These are the feasts of the Lord, holy convocations, which you shall proclaim at their appointed times. On the fourteenth day of the first month at twilight is the Lord's Passover." Leviticus 23:4-5

The Passover Feast or Pesach Feast commemorated Israel's deliverance from Egypt to the Promised Land. It was a celebration of both freedom and hope for Israel. The unleavened bread symbolized Christ's body; the wine signified Christ's blood, and the bitter herbs symbolized the bitter lives Israel had in Egypt. On Passover, Israel was to think about the Egyptian bondage they had been in and how God delivered them from the slavery. The Passover was the only holiday God told Israel to pass down to their children for all generations. The Passover was also a reminder that no matter how dark the situation looked, there was always hope and redemption. The Passover was a seven-day festival in which Israel was to refrain from eating leavened bread or having it in their homes. Israel was to slaughter a lamb on the afternoon of the fourteenth of the Hebrew month of Nisan (March or April), eating it as a festive meal and retelling the story of Passover.

"Now the blood shall be a sign for you on the houses where you are. And when I see the blood, I will pass over you; and the plague shall not be on you to destroy you when I strike the land of Egypt." Exodus 12:13

Matzah is Hebrew for unleavened bread, which was eaten during the Passover. The unleavened bread speaks of holiness, as Christ was the Holy Lamb. We need holiness to maintain fellowship with God in prayer. The unleavened bread also represented poverty and freedom and was eaten as a symbol of the haste in which Israel left Egypt. When they finally left Israel, they left in a hurry and didn't have time to allow their bread to rise. Thus, on Passover, "unrisen" bread was eaten to signify the haste.

Matzah bread had a spiritual significance, signifying humility, as well as a symbol of rejecting arrogance. Just as bread rises, we become "swelled" with pride and arrogance, if we don't guard against that happening.

Just before Jesus was taken to be our Passover Lamb on the cross, He celebrated the Passover with the disciples. As they were eating, Jesus took the bread, blessed and broke it, and gave it to the disciples and said, "Take, eat: this signifies My body." Matthew 26:26

Then He took the cup, and gave thanks, and gave it to them, saying, "Drink from it, all of you. For this is My blood of the new covenant, which is shed for many for the remission of sins." Matthew 26:27-28

"Therefore purge out the old leaven, that you may be a new lump, since you truly are unleavened. For indeed Christ, our Passover, was sacrificed for us. Therefore let us keep the feast, not with old leaven, nor with the leaven of malice and wickedness, but with the unleavened bread of sincerity and truth." I Corinthians 5:7-8

Even though the death of Jesus had not taken place at this time, Israel was to celebrate the Passover and the other feasts and remember what God had done for them in delivering them from death.

"And on the fifteenth day of the same month is the Feast of the Unleavened Bread to the Lord; seven days you must eat unleavened bread. On the first day you shall have a holy convocation; you shall do no customary work on it. But you shall offer an offering made by fire to the Lord for seven days. The seventh day shall be a holy convocation; you shall do no customary work on it." Leviticus 23:6-8

<u>The Feast of Unleavened Bread</u> was celebrated for seven days, directly after the Passover Feast, on the fifteenth day of the month of Nisan at twilight. All leaven was taken out of the home by noon of the fourteenth, and the sacrificial lamb was slain in the afternoon of the fourteenth. Israel was to eat the roasted lamb and bitter herbs and unleavened bread, as on the night of the Passover in Egypt. They were to eat the unleavened bread for seven days, and no work was performed on the first and seventh day of the celebration. They were to make an offering by fire to God each of the seven days. Again, the unleavened bread spoke of holiness and we need holiness as we maintain fellowship with God. Fellowship was established on the basis of the applied blood and we maintain fellowship, as we walk in holiness with Christ.

And the Lord spoke to Moses, saying, Speak to the children of Israel, and say to them: "When you come into the Land which I give to you, and reap its harvest, then you shall bring a sheaf of the first fruits of your harvest to the priest. He shall wave the sheaf before the Lord, to be accepted on your behalf; on the day after the Sabbath the priest shall wave it. And you shall offer on that day, when you wave the sheaf, a male lamb of the first year, without blemish, as a burnt offering to the Lord. Its grain offering shall be two tenths of an ephah of fine flour mixed with oil, an offering made by fire to the Lord, for a sweet aroma; and its drink offering shall be of wine, one-fourth of a hin. You shall eat neither bread nor parched grain nor fresh grain until the same day that you have brought an offering to your God; it shall be a statute forever throughout your generations in all your dwellings." Leviticus 23:9-14

The Feast of First Fruits or the Day of Pentecost and the Feast of Weeks or Shavuot is linked together as agricultural feasts. Waving an omer, which was the best of the year's produce, indicated the first fruits of the barley harvest.

For the Feast of Weeks two loaves of bread were made, using the wheat from the wheat crop as the "First Fruit" of the Shavuot. Waving the two loaves of bread on Pentecost indicated the first fruits of the wheat harvest. The omer was mixed with oil and frankincense and was given for a sweet aroma before the Lord. The oil was symbolic of the holy spirit, and frankincense was symbolic of communion with God through prayer.

These two occasions were bound together by counting a certain number of days from the first event to the second event because Shavuot is not given a certain date to observe.

The Shavuot could not be observed without the waving of the omer and was celebrated after the Feast of the First Fruits. One was not observed without the other.

"And you shall count for yourselves from the day after the Sabbath, from this day that you brought the sheaf of the wave offering: seven Sabbaths shall be completed. Count fifty days to the day after the seventh Sabbath; then you shall offer a new grain offering to the Lord. You shall bring from your dwellings two wave loaves of two-tenths of an ephah. They shall be of fine flour; they shall be baked with leaven. They are the first fruits to the Lord. And you shall offer with the bread seven lambs of the first year, without blemish, one young bull and two rams. They shall be as a burnt offering to the Lord, with their grain offering and their drink offering, an offering made by fire for a sweet aroma to the Lord. Then you shall sacrifice one kid of the goats as a sin offering, and two male lambs of the first year as a sacrifice of a peace offering. The priest shall wave them with the bread of the first fruits as a wave offering before the Lord, with the two lambs. They shall be holy to the Lord for the priest. And you shall proclaim on the same day that it is a holy convocation to you. You shall do no customary work on it. It shall be a statute forever in all your dwellings throughout your generations." Leviticus 23:15-21

The Feast of Weeks or Shavuot was observed in the Hebrew month of Sivan, usually in early June. It was the only celebration that was connected to the spring harvest that celebrated the first fruits of the season. It began with the second night of Passover and was an omer or the best of the first fruits. In Exodus 23:15 Shavuot was called the Feast of Weeks because it fell during the wheat harvest season. It was from this wheat that two loaves of bread were made and used as a meal offering. During the daylight hour the two loaves of bread were presented to God at the bronze altar.

The priest stood at the top of the altar on the east side and put his hands under the two loaves. A wave offering and a heave offering were made before the Lord. The wave offering was made by presenting the bread in a horizontal direction. The wave offering signified that God was the Ruler of the earth. The heave offering was presented by an up-and-down motion. The heave offering signified that God was the Ruler of the heaven. The priest would then swing them before the Lord forward, backward, up and down. These loaves were not burned with fire but were shared with the priest for nourishment. Shavuot was a two-day holiday, and it commemorated the giving of the Torah on Mount Sinai by God. The Torah was the essence of Israel's faith and was the key to connecting Israel for all generations.

Then the Lord spoke to Moses, saying, "Speak to the children of Israel, saying: In the seventh month, on the first day of the month, you shall have a Sabbath-rest, a memorial of blowing of trumpets, a holy convocation. You shall do no customary work on it; and you shall offer an offering made by fire to the Lord." Leviticus 23:23-25

The Feast of Trumpets or Rosh Hashanah was the holiest time of the year. It was the beginning of the Jewish New Year, celebrated on the new moon in the month of Tishri, known to us as September. The festival of Rosh Hashanah was instituted by God and was given to Israel on Mount Sinai.

Yom Kippur and Rosh Hashanah were referred to as the "Days of Awe" or "Days of Fear." Each person would come face-to-face with how little power he had over

110

his life. During Rosh Hashanah, Israel was being judged for its behavior at that time. The Shofar (Ram's Horn) was blown on the holiday of Rosh Hashanah as a memorial. This was to remind Israel of its covenant with God, to encourage its people to have faith in the future New Year and to give them an opportunity to rededicate their lives to God.

The Israelites celebrated Rosh Hashanah and were judged for their behavior, realizing they had no power over their life. That did not change. Through the cross of Calvary, forgiveness was granted along with the knowledge of God's ultimate authority/ control. God's way has always been for us to seek Him daily, being dependant on His help in every situation.

"It shall be to you a Sabbath of solemn rest, and you shall afflict your souls; on the ninth day of the month at evening, from evening to evening, you shall celebrate your Sabbath." Leviticus 23:32

The Day of Atonement or Yom Kippur was celebrated in the Hebrew month of Tishri, September or October. This was the day to seek forgiveness from other people and from God for the wrongs that were committed. On the Day of Atonement, each person was to fast from sundown, marking the beginning of the holiday, to the next evening. Each person was to bring a sacrifice to make atonement for his sins. No one was allowed to do any work on this day. It was to be a "Shabbat" of solemn rest. This was to be an ordinance throughout all the generations for all the people. Israel was to fast and pray for forgiveness of their sins. On this day, the High Priest (Aaron) would wear a specially-made white vestment and cleanse himself with water, and then would begin the purification ritual. The High Priest would take two male goats and place them near the altar to God. One goat was to be a sacrifice to God, while the other goat was a chosen sacrifice for the people. The High Priest was to lay both hands on the goat and confess all the iniquities and transgressions of Israel, putting all the sins on the head of the goat and then sending the goat out into the wilderness, as if to carry away the sins of Israel. This was the only holiday in which the High Priest entered into the "Holy of Holies" and was in God's presence.

And the Lord spoke to Moses, saying: "Also the tenth day of this seventh month shall be the Day of Atonement. It shall be a holy convocation for you; you shall afflict your souls, and offer an offering made by fire to the Lord. And you shall do no work on that same day, for it is the Day of Atonement to make atonement for you before the Lord your God." Leviticus 23:26-28

<u>The Feast of Tabernacles or Sukkot</u> was celebrated on the fifteenth day of the seventh month, Tishri, of the Hebrew calendar. This was in September or October of our calendar. The Sukkot was a celebration of the conclusion of the harvest season. For seven days a burnt offering and a grain offering were to be made by fire before the Lord. No work was done on the first day or the last day of the feast.

All of Israel had been dwelling in booths or "Sukkot" since God had brought them out of Egypt. These booths which encircled the Tabernacle were considered temporary housing for Israel, and they were moved along with Israel. The Sukkah was to have more than two walls and a roof made of organic material such as tree branches or palm fronds. There were not to be enough branches put on top of the Sukkah to block the stars, because the stars were a symbol of God's presence. The Sukkah was to be large enough for anyone to take meals inside and was a symbol of God's protection.

During the celebration of Sukkot, there were candle lighting and blessings over wine, bread and festive food. After the celebration, Israel gathered for the reading of the Torah.

During the feasts, God wanted the Israelites to keep their eyes on Him as they celebrated and worshiped.

How can these feasts be related to prayer?

The primary goal of the Sabbath was for the Israelites to focus on their faith. That set an example/pattern for us to keep our focus on faith in God through prayer.

Israel was delivered from Egypt and the Passover was a celebration of freedom and hope. Christ bought our freedom and the hope that He would do all He said He would do through prayer and His word.

The unleavened bread spoke of holiness, and holiness has always been a condition necessary for maintaining fellowship with God. Holiness, reverence, and awe were set forth as requirements for coming to God.

The Matzah bread had a spiritual significance of humility. God has always emphasized having an attitude of humility.

The oil was symbolic of the Holy Spirit. The Holy Spirit came on the Day of Pentecost (which is when the first church began) to guide and direct us in our every day life.

The frankincense was symbolic of communion with God. According to Revelation 8:4, frankincense was mixed with the prayers of the saints, and ascended before God from the angel's hand, for a sweet-smelling savor to God.

As the Torah was the essence of Israel's faith, our Bible and our salvation through faith in Jesus Christ has been our foundation through the ages.

The Rosh Hashanah was given to remind the Israelites of their covenant with God and encourage them to have faith in the future. Jesus gave us a New Covenant to encourage our faith.

On the Day of Atonement the Israelites asked forgiveness for their sins from each other and from God. The instructions in the Lord's Prayer told us to forgive, as we are forgiven.

God showed the Israelites over and over again how He loved them, and wanted to provide for them, and to use them. He has not changed; His heart has always yearned for us to respond to Him in the same way a child responds to a loving father, with trust and confidence, knowing his "Daddy" will take care of things!

8

A NEW BEGINNING

The land of Canaan was also called the Promised Land. It was called the Promised Land because it was a land flowing with milk and honey. God expected the Israelites to obey His leading, even if it meant removing obstacles that were in their way. And there were plenty of obstacles to be overcome as the Israelites prepared to enter the Promised Land.

Moses sent out twelve spies to check out the land. Two of the ten spies (Joshua and Caleb) came back with a positive report. They knew that the Israelites could defeat the giants in the Promised Land with God's help. They believed God and believed in His mighty power.

Ten of the twelve spies came back and reported that it was truly a land flowing with milk and honey, but they also acknowledged giants that would need to be defeated. The ten spies were extremely negative in their report, feeling the Israelites could not overcome the obstacles that were in their way. They were looking at Israel and her weakness, instead of looking to God and His greatness.

They were walking by sight, not by faith. Faith looks ahead with courage, whereas unbelief looks back with complaining. Faith unites people to God, and unbelief looks for someone to blame. Faith brings life, and unbelief brings defeat and death. Unbelief wastes time and makes God look like a liar, questioning the dependability of His word. Because of unbelief, what would have been an eleven-day journey took the Israelites forty years to accomplish. Israel's unbelief robbed them of God's best for them.

The ten spies and all the people twenty years old or older died because of their unbelief. Unbelief can blind us to God's truth, power and greatness, and it magnifies our weakness. We need to remember that with God, all things are possible. If God gives us a work to do, we need to remember that it is a divine vocation from God, and we need to do it to bring glory to Him. Whenever we are tempted to complain about things we don't agree with, let us reflect on Israel and see how we need to look to God and not on the situation or each other.

God continued to be in control as He led the people, even to the extent of denying Moses and Aaron entrance into the Promised Land. This shows God's power did not depend on either great leader.

Moses took Aaron and his son Eleazar up on Mount Hor and Aaron gave Eleazar his priestly garments. Eleazar was to be the next High Priest for Israel. Aaron died on Mount Hor before Israel reached the Promised Land. God never allowed Aaron to go into the Promised Land because of his rebellion against God's word in Meribah.

God told Moses to go up onto Mount Abarim and see the land flowing with milk and honey, which He was going to give the children of Israel. Moses was not going into the land because he smote the rock with his rod in Meribah instead of speaking to the rock as God told him. When God gives instructions, He wants us to follow them exactly. God also told Moses to gather the congregation of Israel together and to bring Joshua and lay hands on him and inaugurate him as the new leader.

Israel, as a nation, was about to go into transition. They had wandered about for forty years in the wilderness. Now their descendants were ready to settle down in a new land, transitioning from Moses to Joshua as their new leader, and from Aaron to Eleazar as Priest.

Moses carried out God's instructions to teach the people and prepare them to enter the Promised Land. God repeated the commandments to the people of Israel, wanting them to remember Him and His statutes. God wanted Israel to teach its children His laws for obedience.

Israel, as a nation, had experienced important victories. Now their children were about to inherit a new homeland. But God wanted them to remember where they had come from. He wanted Israel to remember His protection, His provisions and believe that He would continue to provide for all their needs.

To obey God's laws and to submit to His will result in spiritual prosperity. Disobedience and rejection result in judgment, poverty and death.

"Whatever I command you, be careful to observe it; you shall not add to it nor take away from it." Deuteronomy 12:32

God reminded Israel of the laws He had given them to help them keep their priorities and to rule the nation. God knows standing for truth is not easy and He promised to be with His people to bring victory. He wanted Israel to have blessings of obedience, not curses of disobedience.

God wants our life to be marked with obedience and integrity. To choose Satan's way over God's way brings emptiness, pain and death. To choose God's way brings blessings and a fulfilled life.

Moses told Joshua to:

"Be strong and of good courage; do not be afraid, nor be dismayed, for the Lord your God is with you wherever you go." Joshua 1:9

Joshua led the children of Israel into the Promised Land. There were many battles they had to fight. But with God's help, they became victorious. The twelve tribes conquered the land, and God rewarded Israel with the homeland.

After Joshua died, new leadership took over. The new generation ignored the moral values and neglected God's laws. Their values began to disappear, and the morals of the people declined. This brought disaster to Israel. They started to worship false gods again and suffered foreign invasion and devastation.

They turned back to God for a while but had a real struggle. God had formed them into a nation, and He was calling them and all believers today to be a kingdom of priests and kings. They had a hard time grasping that concept.

Pride and selfishness have always been and still are a reason for conflict. We want our way, and our way is the correct way to our thinking. Satan loves this attitude. That is why we need to keep our guard up against Satan and put on our armor every day.

We need to ask God for forgiveness for any wrong we may have done in any situation. Only He can show us what we can do to avoid conflict. One of the worst problems associated with conflict is gossiping about the situation and about how we were wronged. In any conflict, we need to seek God and wait on Him to work things out for His good and the good of all involved. This is true even when we don't know what is happening. Conflict starts with a selfish desire.

Therefore, we need to have faith that God will see us through no matter what the situation may be. There is a reason for all things, and we need to learn to grow from our experiences through faith.

Having faith is the secret to a godly life and standing firm with God at our side, knowing He will never leave us nor forsake us.

"Where do wars and fights come from among you? Do they not come from your desires for pleasure that war in your members? James 4:1

When we have a problem with someone or something, it is because our expectations are not being met. It is not wrong to desire things like peace, love, contentment, respect or other good things. But if we fight to achieve our desires and expect another person to cater to us, that is wrong. One of the problems in conflict is that one or both parties feel superior to another person. That is another source of pride. Then we may start to criticize the other person verbally to others, condemning them and allowing bitterness and hatred to enter our hearts. This reveals a lack of love for the other person and judgment toward the other person, but also a lack of faith in God.

When people fail to do as we think they should, sometimes we want to get revenge by making them pay for what they have done to us. We may lash out verbally or think of a devious act to do to them. This is certainly not God's way. If we see ourselves doing these things, we need to pray and ask God to reveal to us the evil in our heart. With God's help, we can overcome our lack of love for others.

There are certain questions we may want to ask ourselves: First, we may want to seek God and ask Him what His plan is in this situation. Then we need to be sure we are reacting with the word of God and not with our own feelings. Also: Can I be a positive Christian influence in this situation and will God be glorified? Am I seeking glory or is God receiving the glory? Am I responding responsibly and is my thinking reasonable and realistic? Is this God's will, and do I have a peace about it? Sometimes it is better not to discuss conflict with others to be sure we are not gossiping. But, there is wisdom in seeking godly council. How can I help someone else through this conflict? Can I grow and become more godly? Go to God and allow Him to show you what He wants for you to do in this situation. And of course, we are looking again at forgiveness. God commands us to forgive one another, even if it is extremely hard.

In the past, I had a problem trying to forgive someone, and I kept asking God to do it through me because I couldn't do it alone. It took about two years, but one day I knew I had forgiven that person. I didn't do anything except ask God to do it through me and He did. Notice, I was willing to forgive but felt unable to forgive. Being willing to forgive is an act of our will. So if you have a problem with forgiveness, continue to pray daily until you see deliverance, as God is always faithful.

9

BEIT YAHWEH

(The House of God)

As King David lay on his death bed, he instructed his son and heir to the throne, Solomon, to obey God's Laws and to follow God, as this was the key to prosperity. Solomon became the next king over Israel.

In a dream, the Lord asked Solomon, "What shall I give you?" Solomon asked for wisdom so that he would have an understanding heart to judge the people and to discern between good and evil. The Lord granted his wish. (I Kings 3:9)

Not long after King Solomon became king, he prepared to build a Temple for the people of Israel in Jerusalem. King David had wanted to build a Temple for Israel, but God would not allow it because David was a man of war and had blood on his hands. King

David had accumulated most of the material for the Temple, but King Solomon built the Temple on Mount Moriah, taking seven years.

King Hiram, the King of Tyre from Lebanon, supplied the timber and the work force to be used to build the Temple. King Solomon demonstrated wisdom and compassion toward the workers as they built the Temple. There were thirty thousand workers used by King Solomon. Consideration for the workers moved him to use only one third of them at a time because they did not live close to the building site.

The plan for the Temple, as well as the Tabernacle, was patterned after God's Temple in heaven. The Temple was double the size of the Tabernacle and was built about 968 BC. God prohibited the use of any iron implements in the building of the Temple.

"And the temple, when it was being built, was built with stone finished at the quarry, so that no hammer or chisel or any iron tool was heard in the temple while it was being built." I Kings 6:7

The Temple was a rectangular structure, approximately one hundred five feet long, thirty feet wide, and forty-five feet high and sat on thirty-five acres of land. Like the Tabernacle, the gate was on the east side, and the Holy of Holies was on the west side of the Temple. The Temple, like the Tabernacle, had three rooms: the porch or vestibule, the nave or Holy Place, and the inner sanctuary or Holy of Holies. The whole building was built of stone on the outside, paneled inside with cedar beams and planks, and carved with ornamental buds and open flowers. The floor was made of planks of cypress. (I Kings 6)

The vestibule or porch was thirty feet wide and fifteen feet deep, serving as a transition room from the front door to the Holy Place. The halls or porches around the court served as a convenient place for interaction for meetings or discussions. (I Kings 6)

The nave or the Holy Place was sixty feet long, thirty feet wide and forty-five feet high. It contained an incense altar made of gold and ten showbread tables. There were five showbread tables on the north wall and five showbread tables on the south wall. There were ten large wooden lampstands overlaid with gold, five on the north side and five on the south side. (I Kings 6)

The inner sanctuary or Holy of Holies was thirty feet long and thirty feet wide. Gold chains were stretched across the inner sanctuary and overlaid with pure gold. Everything was overlaid with pure gold, except the altar was overlaid with cedar. The Ark of the Covenant was placed in the Holy of Holies, with the two small Cherubim placed on the Ark of the Covenant. In addition to the small Cherubim, there were two enormous Cherubim fifteen feet high with wings fifteen feet long that extended to the outer walls. Their wings touched each other in the middle of the room. They were overlaid with gold and were to stand guard over the Ark of the Covenant. (I Kings 6:23-28) The two rooms, the Holy Place and the Holy of Holies were separated by a door, instead of a veil, as was used in the Tabernacle.

All of the walls of the Temple, both the inner and outer sanctuaries, had carved cherubim, palm trees, and open flowers and were overlaid with gold.

The halls and the doors of the Temple had cherubim carved and overlaid with gold, as symbols of guardians of the sacred place.

In the courtyard stood a huge bronze altar fifteen feet high and thirty feet square, where the sacrifices were burnt. Between the altar and the Temple stood a bronze basin called a "Sea" fifteen feet in diameter and seven feet tall. It stood on twelve bronze oxen, three each facing all four directions. (I Kings 7:23-26)

There were ten smaller basins mounted on wheels. Water for washing the burnt offerings came from the smaller basins, while the water from the large basin was used for the washing of the priests' bodies.

Among the furnishings for the Temple were the basins, candle snuffers, ladles, sprinkling bowls, lavers and fire pans, all made of pure gold. All of the furnishings brought into the Temple were made of silver or gold.

After the lavish Temple was constructed, it was a place of Glory once the Glory of the Lord moved in. The Temple was a symbol of Israel's national sovereignty. The dedication ceremony began with a joyful celebration. The people gathered at the front of the Temple, making sacrifices after the Ark of the Covenant was established in the Holy of Holies. The Lord showed His approval of the Temple by making His Presence known with a cloud filling the house of the Lord.

"And it came to pass, when the priests came out of the holy place that the cloud filled the house of the Lord, so that the priests could not continue ministering because of the clouds; for the glory of the Lord filled the house of the Lord." I Kings 8:10-11

King Solomon gave a dedication speech, explaining that the Temple was a dwelling place for God, and that God would continue to be faithful to His people if they would be faithful to Him. King Solomon connected the Temple to the covenant with King David, saying,

"Concerning this Temple which you are building, if you walk in My statutes, execute My judgments, keep all My commandments, and walk in them, then I will perform My word with you which I spoke to your father David. And I will dwell among the children of Israel, and will not forsake My people Israel." I Kings 6:12-13

King Solomon recognized the Temple as a "House of Prayer" for the Israelites. It was a place of blessing and sacrifice. The people were to give their best to the Lord and to share their blessings with others. King Solomon's speech placed emphasis on a heart of personal obedience and loyalty to God. Each one must recognize the condition of his own heart and come back to God if he has strayed.

God's plan for the Temple was for His people to dwell in His Presence. All the Jews in Israel came to Jerusalem to worship, especially for the festivals. The Temple became the sacred sanctuary for Israel. Israel's attention was centered on the Temple, where worship was carried out by the priests from the tribe of Levi. Music was an extremely important part of worship in the Temple, with large choirs of priests trained in instruments and singing. (I Chronicles 25)

After the dedication, King Solomon blessed all the people through prayer and offered a sacrifice of peace offerings with twenty-two thousand bulls and one hundred and twenty thousand sheep. (I Kings 8:63)

Not only did King Solomon build the "House of God" and the wall around Jerusalem, but he also built a palace for himself, which was larger than the Temple and was built next to the Temple. It took thirteen years to build the palace. King Solomon was a man of great wealth, with a fleet of cargo ships, importing and exporting goods to and from Israel. He also had many camels and gold. One of his greatest enterprises was the trading of chariots and horsemen. God had been extremely gracious to him because of his wisdom and his obedience.

King Solomon had a weakness, however, for foreign women. God had told Israel not to intermarry with other nationalities because He knew their hearts would turn away from Him to false gods. But Solomon, in his weakness, didn't listen. Soon, the other wives did turn his heart to other gods. He had seven hundred wives and princesses and three hundred concubines.

Therefore the Lord said to King Solomon,

"Because you have done this and have not kept My covenant and My statutes, which I have commanded you, I will surely tear the kingdom away from you and give it to your servant. Nevertheless I will not do it in your days, for the sake of your father David; I will tear it out of the hand of your son. However, I will not tear away the whole kingdom; I will give one tribe to your son for the sake of My servant David, and for the sake of Jerusalem which I have chosen." I Kings 11:11-13

King Solomon had repaired the damages to the city of David, his father. Jeroboam, his servant, was a young industrious man of valor. King Solomon made him the officer of the labor force of the house of Joseph. Jeroboam went out from Jerusalem and met the prophet Ahijah. Ahijah took the new garment Jeroboam had on and tore it into twelve pieces and told him that God would give him ten tribes of Israel. One tribe would be left for Solomon's son and one tribe would be kept for the sake of Jerusalem. King Solomon and his people had not worshiped God but had worshiped false idols. When King Solomon heard this he tried to kill Jeroboam. Jeroboam fled to Egypt until after King Solomon's death.

King Solomon's practice of idol worship made it difficult for the people to distinguish between right and wrong. Foreign deities were given recognition, and that made it difficult to maintain true worship. The turmoil of the final years of King Solomon's reign and the division of the kingdom were direct results of his involvement in idolatry.

King Solomon reigned in Israel for forty years. He died and was buried in the City of David, which is Jerusalem. His son, Rehoboam, took his place as the next King of Israel. Rehoboam rejected the advice of the experienced elders and listened to his young friends. He abandoned true worship and made a worship of convenience for the people. This resulted in making it easy for the nation to sin.

Israel and Jeroboam, who at the time was an officer of the labor force, refused to accept the ruling of Rehoboam because of his excessive demands for labor and taxes. The once mighty kingdom split into two kingdoms: the Southern Kingdom of Judah with its capital in Jerusalem was ruled by King Rehoboam, and the Northern Kingdom of Israel with its capital in Samaria was ruled by King Jeroboam.

Jeroboam created new Temple centers, complete with his own staff of priests placing golden calves as symbols of "Yahweh," in the Northern Kingdom. They started worshiping Baal and Asherah, false idols. The Northern Kingdom and Temples were destroyed by Assyria in 722 BC.

Hezekiah became King of Judah, following the destruction of the Northern Kingdom. Hezekiah tried to reunite the Northern and Southern Kingdoms to no avail.

Josiah, a later king, centralized religious worship in Jerusalem. In the course of repairing the Temple, a scroll was discovered that threatened the wrath of God on Judah because of the people's disobedience to the covenant. (II Kings 22:1-7)

Because of this discovery, Josiah destroyed all the images made for Baal. God's Presence was withdrawn, leaving Israel and the Temple at risk. King Solomon's Temple had stood for over four hundred years and was burned by Nebuchadnezzar and the Babylonians in 586 BC. And the Temples treasures were plundered, leaving nothing but broken hearts as a result of their sin.

In 539 BC, Cyrus, the Persian King, conquered Babylon and gave Israel permission to return to Jerusalem to rebuild the Temple. In 538 BC Sheshbazzar, the prince of Judah led the first group back to Jerusalem. They carried with them some of the vessels that belonged to the Temple that had been plundered by the Babylonians. They erected an altar, offered sacrifice and started preparation for rebuilding the Temple.

A second group was led by Zerubbabel, and they started to rebuild the Temple, dedicating it in 515 BC. Israel and its children and all the priests dedicated the "House of God" with joy. The Ark of the Covenant and the Cherubim were gone, and the Holy of Holies remained empty. The Bible does not explain why or where the Ark of the Covenant or the Cherubim were.

Zerubbabel's Temple continued to be the focus of Israel. When Nehemiah became Governor, God put it in his heart to rebuild the walls around the Temple. He had much opposition but remained faithful to God. With much prayer and obedience to God, the walls were repaired, and the Temple was safe once again.

Through constant conflict, the Temple was destroyed but replaced by Herod's Temple in 19 BC. King Herod was a descendent of the Edomites, and he had converted to Judaism. His goal was not religion but politics. King Herod was a tyrant ruler, but was famous for renovating the Temple. His goal in renovating the Temple was to try to buy the loyalty of Israel. He started the renovation of the Temple in 19 BC, but it was not completed until AD 63.This was also the Temple in which Jesus preached. King Herod believed the Temple would be such a great task that it would assure his remembrance, which it has. He completely dismantled the old Temple and replaced it with a new structure. King Herod maintained the basic floor plan and the dimensions of the Temple, but enlarged the courtyard by doubling the size of the platform on the Temple Mount. The Temple was one of the most beautiful creations of the ancient world and had excellent engineering.

King Herod's Temple was fifteen hundred fifty feet long and one thousand feet wide. The Temple was near the middle of the inner courtyard facing and surrounded by another wall. Israel could pass through the gate and enter into a square courtyard. Just inside the gate were large chests to collect money. This is where the widow gave her mite, all she had to give. (Luke 21:2-3) Huge lampstands were lit at night to establish safety among the brethren, especially during the feasts. The women stood in the courtyard to watch the sacrifices at the altar and watch the priest participate in worship through prayer, singing and fasting. The men climbed fifteen stairs to enter into a narrow court to watch the priest offer sacrifices from the place where the animals were killed. The priests were behind a bronze laver that provided water fed by an underground cistern. King Herod's Temple had a massive altar in the courtyard for sacrifices and was much larger than the one used in King Solomon's time. As with King Solomon's Temple, this Temple had the Holy Place and the Most Holy Place.

The Most Holy Place was a cubed-shaped room of thirty-four feet in each direction, overlaid with gold. There was a veil in front of the Most Holy Place, but the Ark of the Covenant was gone, so the Most Holy Place was empty.

The Holy Place was one hundred three feet long and thirty-four feet wide and sixty-nine feet high. The Holy Place was completely covered with plates of gold and divided by the veil. The veil that separated the Holy Place from the Most Holy Place was assumed to be the one that was torn in two pieces the moment Christ died on the cross. (Matthew 27:51) The Holy Place had furnishings similar to King Solomon's Temple, with a seven-branch lampstands and a showbread table and an incense altar.

The Temple, once again, became the focal point of conflict between the Romans and the Jews. The Romans came to battle with military force, and they besieged Jerusalem. The Temple was burned to the ground in AD 70. The Jews were forced to develop new ways of religion. For one thousand years, the Temples in Jerusalem had been the heart of the Jewish religion, and this destruction created a great spiritual crisis.

So, therefore, what does this have to do with prayer? The Most Holy Place was where the Presence of God dwelt, in both Temples, as in the Tabernacle. The High Priest would continue to come and pray for the sins of the people once a year.

The Holy Place had the showbread table in both Temples, as in the Tabernacle. The showbread table signified the union of Jesus' divine and human nature together in one person while here on earth. The twelve loaves of bread signified the twelve tribes of Israel. The lampstand was trimmed and lit every morning to signify God as the Light of the world. The altar of incense in front of the veiled Holy of Holies signified the prayers of Israel going up to God. The veil, which was split in two when Christ died on the cross, was the entrance to fellowship with God, by way of Jesus' death on Calvary. Israel worshiped in the Temples as they had worshiped in the Tabernacle, but a bit more lavishly. God heard the cries and petitions of Israel as well as the priests.

How do we, as Christians, connect our prayer life and worship to the way the Israelites worshiped? We bring our petitions to God through Jesus Christ, not through a human priest interceding for us or offering a sacrifice on our behalf. We give of ourselves, our time, talents, and finances, all for the Glory of God.

What is the mindset of many modern-day Christians on prayer? Some believe that God answers prayers for others but will not answer their prayers. Some feel unworthy of God's love. Others feel He really doesn't love us because of our sin: and for that reason, He will not answer our prayers. Some even have a fatalistic attitude of "What's the benefit of praying?"

God does answer prayer, but He also gives to us the responsibility of repenting of sin and wrongdoing, thereby keeping our heart clean and keeping our motives pure. He also expects us to believe/have faith when we pray.

In regard to pure motives, perhaps an example would help. Selfishness often tries to enter into our praying and may prevent us getting an answer to that prayer. For example, suppose a mother asked God to take her child out of a wrong relationship. God knows the motive in that mother's heart. If that mother is praying from an attitude of revenge or wrong feelings that she is experiencing, God sees that. But, if the mother is praying from a standpoint of what is right for the child, and her prayer is backed up by the word of God, then God sees that also and will answer prayer because of her right attitude.

It is important for us to maintain a right attitude in all our dealings with God. It is comforting to remember that He is all-knowing and all-powerful and that His Love, Mercy, and Grace are fresh every morning. As we commune with Him, telling Him of our love for Him, our desire to be like Him enhances our faith. While we know Him as our Friend, it is good to also dwell on the awesomeness of God to maintain a proper attitude/fear/reverence. Agreeing with Him that He wants to hear our cries and petitions builds our own faith. Quoting His promises back to Him reminds us of His word on any given situation and builds our faith as well. For example, when fear or loneliness comes, reminding Him of His word to never leave us or forsake us (Deuteronomy 31:6) helps us to remain calm. Maintaining a right attitude in this way makes heroes of ordinary people.

There is wisdom in coming to God in prayer, but it is not always easy to come to God every day and pray. It is hard work to intercede, sometimes even a sacrifice, but it is worth it. Coming to God purposely, knowing He wants to answer our prayers and to bless us, brings down blessings on us and on the ones we are praying for.

We should be careful what we pray for and how we pray. I have prayed before and meant to ask for one thing. However, in my wording I asked for something a little bit different and got exactly what I had asked for, but not at all what I wanted. Sometimes this can be confusing, but we need to reflect back and think of the words we used in the prayer. God may be answering our request according to what we asked.

It is fine to go to God with requests for ourselves, but we should not make our whole prayer time just about ourselves. Let us think of other people. If you want a successful business, pray for someone else to have a successful business. If you want to be blessed, ask for God's blessings to be on someone else.

Sometimes God will not answer our prayers right away because He may want us to drop an inappropriate request. Or perhaps He wants us to see our request is childish or self-centered. Or He may want us to modify our request. Sometimes He just wants to build character in us with such qualities as patience, endurance, understanding, submission or trust. Waiting for God to answer will test our faith, and He may want our faith to grow.

When we bring our petitions before God, we should realize that our prayers release the power of God. We are all under satanic attack, and Satan will try to distract us and try to keep our minds on other things instead of praying. Satan is our enemy, and every satanic attack is actually a heavenly battle fought here on earth. Satan's real target is God. Satan wants to interfere with our lives and our prayers. Satan would like to destroy God's response to our prayers and make us think God is not listening.

In the book of Daniel, Daniel was praying to God, and Gabriel, an angel, came to tell Daniel that God had already given an answer to his prayer.

"At the beginning of your supplication the command went out, and I have come to tell you, for you are greatly beloved." Daniel 9:23

Satan has already lost the war. It was fought on Calvary, over two thousand years ago. God has the upper hand in the upper room (which is our prayer closet)! If Satan can convince us that God will not answer our prayers, and that God doesn't care, then he has won and we have lost the battle.

If we go to God with a prideful attitude, He may refuse our request. We need to go to Him with humbleness. Our humility equates God's power.

God maintains throughout His word that He is not only our Friend, but our Healer as well, regardless of whether that healing is spiritual, physical, mental or emotional. He takes the standpoint of His omnipotent (all-powerful) love for us, regardless of our past or present circumstances.

Go to God expecting answers. If we go to God half-heartedly and with doubting, or go to Him uncaringly, He will not answer our prayers. Go to God with authority and confidence that He has heard and will answer. Go to Him being precise and specific and go to Him in brokenness. Ask God to point out things in our prayer life that can be obstructing answers. Admitting our faults can help overcome any obstacles in our way. God doesn't answer when we have a faulty relationship with Him or others, harboring unforgiveness or having a bad attitude against others. He won't answer when we pray with wrong motives or for wrong things, or if we don't pray in His will. We must not forget to ask, or quit praying too soon. Never Give Up!

Our attitude in prayer should be one of expectancy. Being lukewarm in our praying, doubting, or lacking compassion can hinder us in our prayers. Praying with the authority He has given us and the confidence that He will hear and answer reaps rewards in prayer. Being precise and specific and approaching Him humbly, not pridefully, will bring answers also.

Daily prayer should make room for personal soul searching/self-examination. Admitting our faults and confessing sin helps to overcome prayer/hindrances/ obstacles. Broken fellowship with Him because of sin, harboring unforgiveness, or bad attitudes (to name a few) can definitely interfere in seeing answered prayer.

Again, we are to be mindful to be persistent in prayer, to have a "never give up" attitude. I have prayed at different times for different people for years for salvation. God has always answered my prayers, and the person I was praying for became saved. I have found that it may take years for God to answer, because the circumstances have to be suitable for the person to accept Christ. God may have to get that person to a certain level in his life, before the prayer can be answered.

We cannot have a close relationship with God if we don't pray. How would you feel if someone you loved never talked to you? You would not feel close to this person, would you? When we fail to talk to God, we lose our love for Him and for others and lose our faith that He can and will answer our prayers. When we are weak in our prayer life, everything we do becomes disproportionate. If we are not hearing from God, could it be He is not hearing from us? If we are disrespectful to God by approving of something that we know is wrong, we will not get answers to our prayers. If we harbor sin and continue to do that sin, and yet we pray, God will not answer.

"But your iniquities have separated you from your God; And your sins have hidden His face from you, So that He will not hear." Isaiah 59:2

When we give our life to Christ, He wants all of our being. He wants access to that secret room we have hidden in our hearts. There is no room for secret sin. You may have a sin that you want no one to find out about, or you may be deceiving yourself into thinking that it doesn't exist. God already knows about it and the Bible says:

"If we say we have no sin, we deceive ourselves, and the truth is not in us. If we confess our sins, He is faithful and just to forgive us our sins and to cleanse us from all unrighteousness. If we say that we have not sinned, we make Him a liar, and His word is not in us." I John 1:8-10

God is perfect, and He cannot lie. If we claim to be without sin, we are deceiving ourselves. That is a lie the devil wants us to believe. If we don't feel that we are sinners, we will not feel we have a need for a Savior. And, Satan will win again; and when we die, we will go to hell.

As Christians, God does not expect us to be perfect, but He does expect us to strive toward perfection. We are to be Christ-like. That is what being a Christian is about.

10

MYTH AMISS

A myth is a traditional narrative, usually involving supernatural or imaginary persons. A myth is also a popular idea widely held about a false or fictitious person, idea or thing.

Many people today turn to tarot cards, palm readers, or Ouija boards. Some people turn to witchcraft or believe in folklore tales or a number of other things instead of believing in the "One True God." These are all part of Satan's schemes. Satan will lead us astray, if we allow it. He wants us to believe in anything, except the truth. Anything or anyone we put our trust in, except God, is a false idol. And a false idol can do nothing for us. If we believe in any object or person and believe that it or they can keep us safe or can guide us and help us along life's path, we are badly mistaken, and Satan is telling us a lie.

God is the only One who can guide and direct our path and perform true miracles. Satan can imitate God, and he wants us to believe that these cards or Ouija boards or whatever else, will bring us truth, guidance and happiness. Satan can tell us things about our future. And he can surely tell us about our past, but he will not guide us correctly because he wants to destroy us.

"The thief does not come except to steal, and to kill, and to destroy. I have come that they may have life, and that they may have it more abundantly." John 10:10

The thief in this passage is Satan, and it is Jesus who will bring life more abundantly. God is the Giver of life and wants to give us an abundant life to the fullest. He is our Guide and Helper and will give us the answer to any problem that comes our way. He does not tell us our future because He wants to protect us from things we could not handle, if we knew ahead of time what trial or trouble would be coming our way.

Religion is the belief and worship of a personal God or superhuman controlling power. Religion is a particular system of faith and worship.

Some people feel religion should be mystical or wrapped up in mystery. God is not a God of confusion or mystery. If we are confused, it is because Satan wants to confuse us so we won't know what to believe. If we turn to false idols, a false idol will not save us from anything.

God has given us the Holy Bible which opens the door to Him and to Heaven. It is our guide to living a life of truth, prosperity, and happiness. True guidance cannot resemble magic or be mystical. Any problem or answer to any question we may have in life is found in the Bible and through prayer to our Father.

God is not a superficial God. He is not shallow. The more we read the Bible, the more we see the depth of the Bible and learn the depth of God.

Spirituality deals with the spirit, usually considered part of religion. Spirituality may contain religious and non-religious practices. A person may say he is spiritual but may not have a relationship with God. Therefore, if this is true, spirituality means nothing. If we say we are spiritual, that could mean we are worshiping a demon, a false idol, or the one true God in Heaven.

How can we relate religion or spirituality to our every day life? If we believe in anything other than God, our belief system has gone awry. If we are praying to anything or anyone or worshiping anything or anyone besides the God in Heaven, we are worshiping a false idol, and our religion or spirituality is headed in the wrong direction.

Just as Israel worshiped false idols, such as the golden calf, this only got them in trouble. The golden calf could do nothing for them. Why do we feel we have a need to see our God? If we are children of God, we don't have to see Him we know He is real; He is in our heart. We all have a soul. When we are saved, God sends the Holy Spirit down to dwell in our heart, and we have God's word to help guide and direct our path. So we know without a shadow of a doubt that we have an everlasting God who can do all things for us.

In I Timothy, Paul wrote Timothy a letter warning the church in Ephesus against false doctrines and Jewish myths. He wanted the teachers to teach sound doctrine from God's laws, not fictitious stories based on vague genealogical points.

"As I urged you when I went into Macedonia-remain in Ephesus that you may charge some that they may teach no other doctrine. Nor give heed to fables and endless genealogies, which cause disputes rather than godly edification which is in faith." I Timothy 1:3-4

God's word is based on faith. That is as true today as it was then. When we accept Christ, it is through faith. When we work for God's kingdom, it is through faith. Our life should be one of faith in God, and belief in what He says in His word. We should trust in His word, knowing He will see us through. Faith believes something for which there is no proof.

"Now faith is the substance of things hoped for, the evidence of things unseen." Hebrews 11:1

Why go to God in prayer if we don't believe God will answer? If we do, we are going with wrong motives. That is when we need faith.

I had a friend with ovarian cancer who called me one day and asked me to pray for her to have a colostomy reversal. I told her I would pray for her, and I did pray. I will have to admit though, I really didn't think God would grant her wish. Well, a few weeks later, she called me all excited, saying that she was getting the colostomy reversal. God showed me! Where was my faith? That has taught me a valuable lesson, that God answers prayers, even if we don't have the faith of a mustard seed!

So Jesus said to them, "Because of your unbelief, for assuredly, I say to you, if you have faith as a mustard seed, you will say to this mountain, "Move from here to there," and it will move; and nothing will be impossible for you." Matthew 17:20

I feel God answered my friend's prayer because she believed He would answer. If I had been the only one praying, He might not have answered because I didn't have the faith that He would answer. We all need the faith that is available to us as believers. This means believing in a lifestyle of faith, determined that we are going to believe. If we don't believe God will answer, why should He? Prayer does not change things; God does!

Through prayer and study of the Bible, we learn more about God, about faith in God and His word. If we are not sure what a passage says, we should look in a Bible Commentary or another source to help us learn more of what we are studying, or we need to study with other believers. The more we study the Bible, the more we learn about God, and learn to trust Him more. God has given us the Holy Spirit to guide us in learning the truth and knowing what is correct.

The more studying we do, the more we see how God has planned everything for us. He gives us the guide on how we should act, how to prosper, how we should treat others, and how to live a holy life.

Through prayer and God speaking to us through the Holy Spirit, we can see that God is all that His word says and that He wants to answer our prayers. God is a God of love and longs to work in our lives according to what we need. He works in our lives through our faith, giving us hope and loving us enough to see us through all the hardships of life.

"And now abide faith, hope and love, these three; but the greatest of these is love." I Corinthians 13:13

With our faith and hope in God we need to watch how we react to the circumstances in our churches. We should beware of petty arguments in the church. They lead to destruction of the body of Christ. We should beware of thinking more about little things that really don't matter and think instead of edifying the body of Christ. Whatever we do, we need to give God all the glory and praise. Without love for one another and love for God, it is easy to become disgruntled and start to complain.

"Therefore, whether you eat or drink, or whatever you do, do all to the glory of God." I Corinthians 10:31

We have been bought with a price, and we are not our own. Our goal should be to please God, not ourselves. Even if we see someone doing something we would not do, leave it alone. God may be working on them and we may not see "God's Kingdom Plan." We should be building each other up, not tearing each other down. God's overall plans are not shaped by the small things but by things such as peace, righteousness, love and fellowship.

I have heard of churches being torn up because of the congregation arguing over the color of the carpet or some other trivial matter. Let us not be guilty of arguing over such a matter. Is this not idol worship? Are we thinking more highly of the carpet or some other trivial matter than we are God? We can make anything into an idol. And it is all because of selfishness. We are thinking about ourselves and what we want instead of what God wants or other people and their needs. Prayer is the foundation of any church. We should be praying for our pastor, our leaders, and our members. Without prayer, no church will stand.

What are some of the myths surrounding prayer? Some people feel they are not worthy of God listening to their prayers, or that He hears but doesn't want to answer their prayers. Some people don't believe there is a God, so they have no need of Him to answer prayers. Some people have no clue they are a sinner or that they need forgiveness or need an answer to a prayer. Some people feel they have gotten along fine without God all these years, so why do they need Him now? Some people feel God really can't answer their prayers. These are Satan's lies, telling us we have no need for God or that He doesn't exist. Satan is the father of lies and wants us to believe him instead of God.

Another supposed myth surrounding prayer is the fact that Jesus was born in a manger over two thousand years ago. He walked on earth and performed miracles and died on a cross and arose again after three days. These are facts, not myths. The Bible is as real today as it was when it was written over two thousand years ago.

Wake Up! There is a heaven and a hell. They do exist; and without God, we have no hope and will spend eternity in hell.

"Nevertheless do not rejoice in this, that the spirits are subject to you, but rather rejoice because your names are written in heaven." Luke 10:20

Our salvation is more important than the power to overcome Satan or to escape his harm. Our salvation is recorded in heaven, if we have accepted Christ as our Savior!

Is your name written there?

11

ANGELS, GOD'S HEAVENLY HOST

Angels are messengers of God and have been called into existence by God and were all created through Him and for Him. Angels were created to worship and praise God and attend to His creation. Angels have no physical body but can have an appearance of a visible form. They may look like human beings and have a personality, but they are celestial beings corresponding to the spiritual nature of God. Angels were created to be holy but not omniscient, omnipotent, or omnipresent. Only God is all-knowing, all-powerful and all-present. The word angel or some form of an angel has been mentioned in the Old Testament and New Testament. Angels can appear as men, but they never appear as women, nor do they marry or are given in marriage. There are angels around God's throne and they are always watching God's face and listening for an assignment to guard or help one of God's children, deliver messages, or do battle with other spiritual beings on our behalf. They are ready to serve God at any time and in any way. Angels have access to earth to perform the assignments of God.

Long before God created the world, He created angels. The only ones to witness the creation, as far as we know, were the morning stars and sons of God. That is not to say they were the only angels in existence, but they were the ones mentioned in scripture.

There are angels called Seraphim. Seraphim were present at the giving of the Law of Moses; they were present at the birth and resurrection of Christ; they were present at the ascension of Jesus and will come with Jesus when He comes to gather His saints at the second coming. Seraphim are concerned with the holiness of God and stand above God. Isaiah saw the seraphim in the Temple of God.

"I saw the Lord sitting on a throne, high and lifted up, and the train of His robe filled the temple. Above it stood seraphim; each one had six wings: with two he covered his face, with two he covered his feet, and with two he flew. And one cried to another and said: Holy, holy, holy is the Lord of hosts; the whole earth is full of His glory!" Isaiah 6:1-3

The human eye cannot see an angel unless God intervenes and allows one to do so. Angels are ministering spirits to us, so therefore, they can see us.

There was a Seraphim angel named Lucifer. Lucifer was so beautiful that it caused his heart to be lifted up in pride and caused him to want God's position. Under Lucifer's influence, one third of all the angels rebelled and sinned against God. Angels cannot die, but God disqualified the one third from their position of being holy angels. That is when God changed Lucifer's name and he became known as Satan. Seraphim are the root word for serpent. Satan came into the Garden of Eden as a serpent.

What made the angels rebel against God? The Bible doesn't say what made them rebel or how long it took Lucifer to convince the other angels to rebel. After the rebellion of the angels, God decided to create the earth as we know it now and make man in His image, giving us the privilege to accept Him or reject Him.

After God had created the sons of God and they had become fallen angels, they came down to earth and took wives for themselves with the daughters of men and produced giants.

"Now it came to pass, when men began to multiply on the face of the earth, and daughters were born to them, that the sons of God saw the daughters of men, that they were beautiful, and they took wives for themselves of all whom they chose." Genesis 6:1-2

God cast the angels who married the daughters of men into hell, and they are bound with chains because of their wickedness.

"And the angels who did not keep their proper domain, but left their own abode, He has reserved in everlasting chains under darkness, for the judgment of the great day." Jude 1:6

The other fallen angels and Satan were cast into the first heaven, which is earth.

"And war broke out in heaven; Michael and his angels fought with the dragon; and the dragon and his angels fought, but they did not prevail, nor was a place found for them in heaven any longer. So the great dragon was cast out, that serpent of old, called the Devil and Satan, who deceives the whole world; he was cast to the earth, and his angels were cast out with him." Revelation 12:7-9

Satan and his demons are the demons of the world; they are trying to destroy God's people and God's world. At the end of the seven year Tribulation period, Satan and his demonic angels of this world will be cast into hell, which is a lake of fire.

The activities of the holy angels toward the unbelievers are basically activities of judgment. Satan and his demonic angels also exercise activities toward the unbelievers. Satan is the prince of this world and is the spiritual father to the unsaved. Satan tries to prevent the unbelievers from becoming saved by telling them lies. He wants them to believe that God's word is not true. He wants to blind their eyes to the truth of God and close their ears so they will not hear the truth. Satan has his angels devise false doctrine by using false teachers to proclaim lies, so the unbelievers will not know the truth from lies. Satan knows the Bible and will twist it so as to lead people astray. Satan is the master of half-truths.

God gave the angels a free spirit and freedom of choice, as He has us. It was their choice to obey God or not to obey.

Was salvation provided for fallen angels? Salvation was not provided for fallen angels because Jesus became a man and walked on earth for all mankind and died as a substitute for human beings. God provided salvation for all fallen humans, not fallen angels. Christ had not taken on the form of an angel to die on the cross; He took on the form of a man.

"Who, being in the form of God, did not consider it robbery to be equal with God, but made Himself of no reputation, taking the form of a bondservant, and coming in the likeness of men. And being found in appearance of a man, He humbled Himself and became obedient to the point of death, even the death of the cross." Philippians 2:6-8

Satan's pride, lust, greed, vanity, self-centeredness and hatred caused the error of ugliness instead of beauty. Satan tries to imitate God but cannot be God. Satan is the author of confusion and darkness, and God is the Author of light and truth. Light enhances beauty and exposes evil, and darkness hides both.

Why did Satan think he could defeat God? It was his pride. Satan was a beautiful angel, and because of his beauty, he became prideful. Satan could not dethrone God, but he wanted to do everything in his power to defy God's authority. And Satan is still trying to defy God's authority as well as thwart God's plans and harass God's people. Satan cannot read our minds, but he has learned by our actions and our speech what we are thinking. He can react accordingly. That is why we, as Christians, need to keep up our guard and put on our armor every morning.

When Jesus walked on earth, Satan tested Him, trying to dethrone Him and to take His position. Satan used the same method on Jesus that he had used in the Garden of Eden on Adam and Eve. He was successful in the Garden of Eden with Eve but was unsuccessful with Jesus.

The first temptation Satan used appealed to the flesh. Satan told Eve that it was fine for her to eat from the Tree of Knowledge of the Good and Evil that God didn't mean she would die but that she would be like Him. (Genesis 3:4-5) Eve bought into the lies of Satan, unlike Jesus. When Satan tempted Jesus, he told Him if He were the Son of God, He could turn the stones into bread to satisfy His hunger. (Matthew 4:3) Jesus responded,

"Man shall not live by bread alone, but by every word that proceeds from the mouth of God." Matthew 4:4

Again, Satan tried to tempt Jesus with the lust of the eyes. Eve had seen the fruit that was pleasing to the eye and failed the temptation. (Genesis 3:6)

Satan told Jesus if He was the Son of God He could jump from the Pinnacle of the Temple and the angels would catch Him. (Matthew 4:5) Jesus responded,

"You shall not tempt the Lord your God." Matthew 4:7

The third time Satan tried to tempt the Lord with the pride of life. He tried to appeal to His ego. He took Jesus upon a high mountain and showed Him the kingdom. He told Jesus he would give Him the kingdom if He would bow down and worship him.

Satan was showing Jesus a worldly kingdom which had been turned over to the devil at Adam's fall. Jesus replied,

"Away with you, Satan! For it is written: You shall worship the Lord your God, and Him only you shall serve." Then the devil left Him, and behold, the angels came and ministered to Him." Matthew 4:10-11

Jesus was tempted by Satan, but He never bought into Satan's lies. Satan never dethrone Jesus, and he never will.

There are several different kinds of angels and two-thirds of the angels are righteous and holy and worship and serve God, including Michael and Gabriel.

Michael is the archangel and was called the Chief Prince according to Daniel 10:13. He is likely to be the head of all the holy angels. Most holy angels are called the elect angels. Michael is the defender angel who does battle and is called the warrior angel.

Gabriel was an angel of enunciation which means to pronounce clearly. He was sent to proclaim important messages.

When God created the earth, the angels shouted for joy, according to Job. The angels are in the Bible to show us their importance and how they helped the people in the Bible Age. There are many times throughout the Bible when God sent an angel to be a messenger to proclaim good news or to send out a warning to protect the person. Angels were active in the announcement and birth of Christ and attended to His every need.

Before Christ was born, the angel Gabriel was sent by God to the town of Nazareth, in Galilee. Then the angel said to Mary, "Do not be afraid, Mary, for you have found favor with God. And behold, you will conceive in your womb and bring forth a Son, and shall call His name Jesus." Luke 1:30-31

After Mary gave birth to Jesus, the angels ministered to Joseph (Mary's husband and Jesus' earthly Father) in a dream.

After the three kings came and worshiped the baby Jesus, they returned to their country. An angel of the Lord appeared to Joseph in a dream and said:

"Arise and take the young Child and His mother, flee to Egypt and stay there until I bring you word; for Herod will seek the young Child to destroy Him." Matthew 2:13

The angels were standing by, ready to deliver Jesus as a child from Herod. The holy angels were with Christ, while He was here on earth, as He withstood every possible mental, physical, and spiritual hardship that could come upon man. They were also ready to deliver Him from the cross, had they been allowed. After Jesus' death on the cross, an angel came and rolled back the stone to show the believers that He had risen.

"And behold, there was a great earthquake; for an angel of the Lord descended from heaven, and came and rolled back the stone from the door, and sat on it." Matthew 28:2

As Christ ascended into heaven, two stood by to announce to the world that He would return. Christ is going to return, and we need to be ready.

Another type of angel is the cherubim. The name cherub signifies the power of God. In the Holy of Holies of the Tabernacle and the Temple, were two cherubim on top of the Mercy Seat. When Aaron, the High Priest, went in with the sacrifice once a year, he heard the sound of the wings of the cherubim in the outer court before he entered the Holy of Holies. It was like the voice of God Almighty when He speaks.

"Then the glory of the Lord went up from the cherub, and paused over the threshold of the temple; and the house was filled with the cloud, and the court was full of the brightness of the Lord's glory. And the sound of the wings of the cherubim was heard as far as the outer court like the voice of Almighty God when He speaks." Ezekiel 10:4-5

There were cherubim that faced each other on the Ark of the Covenant, and it only talks about one face.

"And the cherubim shall stretch out their wings above, covering the mercy seat with their wings, and they shall face one another; the faces of the cherubim shall be toward the mercy seat." Exodus 25:20

The cherubim in this passage talks about the cherubim having four faces and defend God's holiness from any defilement of sin.

"Also from within it came the likeness of four living creatures. And this was their appearance: they had the likeness of a man. Each one had four faces, and each one had four wings. Their legs were straight, and the soles of their feet were like the soles of calves' feet. They sparkled like the color of burnished bronze. The hands of a man were under their wings on their four sides; and each of the four had faces and wings. Their wings touched one another. The creatures did not turn when they went, but each one went straight forward. As for the likeness of their faces, each of the four had the face of a man; each of the four had the face of a lion on the right side, each of the four had the face of an ox on the left side, and each of the four had the face of an eagle. Thus were their faces. Their wings stretched upward; two wings of each one touched one another, and two covered their bodies. And each one went straight forward; they went wherever the spirit wanted to go, and they did not turn when they went ." Ezekiel 1:5-12

In the throne room of God are four cherubim. The four living creatures, each having six wings, were full of eyes around and within. And they do not rest day or night, saying:

"Holy, holy, holy, Lord God Almighty, Who was, and is and is to come!" Revelation 4:8

The angels are giving honor and glory to the Lord God Almighty. God's power and glory are extended from the past to the eternity yet to come. In Psalms, it says that He sits enthroned between the cherubim.

"The Lord reigns, let the peoples tremble! He dwells between the cherubim; let the earth be moved!" Psalm 99:1

There are angels called thrones or dominions, which could mean enthroned angels. They are used to emphasize the dignity and authority in government. They have also been called wheels of fire, covered with many eyes.

"I watched till thrones were put in place, And the Ancient of Days was seated; His garment was white as snow, And the hair of His head was like pure wool. His throne was a fiery flame, Its wheels a burning fire." Daniel 7:9

The expression of thrones, principalities, dominions, virtues, and powers apply to all angels, whether fallen or holy angels, but usually referring to celestial beings.

"For by Him all things were created that are in heaven and that are on earth, visible and invisible, whether thrones or dominions or principalities or powers. All things were created through Him and for Him." Colossians 1:16

Jesus, as God's Son who walked on earth, is exalted above the angels:

" When He had by Himself purged our sins, sat down at the right hand of the Majesty on high, having become so much better than the angels, as He has by inheritance obtained a more excellent name than they." Hebrews 1:3-4

Many people want to know if we have guardian angels watching over us. We do have angels directed by God to help us in our time of need.

"Are they not all ministering spirits sent forth to minister for those who will inherit salvation?" Hebrews 1:14

The angels watch the face of God day and night and listen for His voice, so as to hear His command to help His children in time of need. If we commit ourselves to God, He will command His angels to take charge over us.

"Take heed that you do not despise one of these little ones, for I say to you that in heaven their angels always see the face of My Father who is in heaven." Matthew 18:10

"Because you have made the Lord, who is my refuge, Even the Most High, your dwelling place, No evil shall befall you, Nor shall any plague come near your dwelling; For He shall give His angels charge over you, To keep you in all your ways." Psalm 91:9-11

How do we connect angels with our lives and prayer? We do not connect angels with our lives; God sends angels to us, to watch and care for us. We <u>do not</u> pray to the angels. Angels cannot help us if we come to them in prayer. They will not listen to us if we pray to them; they are watching and listening for God's voice to tell them what to do. They are in and around the throne room to worship and give honor to God. God does send an angel or many angels in our time of need to help us, to protect us or to warn us of danger. Angels must never replace God in our lives, and angels should never receive worship from us.

The Bible speaks of entertaining angels unaware. We may be in the presence of an angel sometime without actually knowing it. There may be an angel among us, when we least expect it.

"Do not forget to entertain strangers, for by doing so some have unwittingly entertained angels." Hebrews13:2

In my own life, I have had a couple of incidents when I felt angels had helped me out of a bad situation. I'm sure they are there to help me every day; I just don't feel them.

One day I was in my mother's storage room outside her home. There was a gas stove in the room with a flame flickering up. When I went back outside, I realized I was too warm. I turned my head to one side and saw flames flickering up my back. I pulled my sweater and turtle neck, which the fire had already burned into, over my head. After I threw the clothes on the ground, I stomped the flames out. I felt there possibly was an angel or several angels that helped me get my clothes off without getting my hair or face on fire. After I realized what could have happened, I thanked God for His protective hand on me.

Another time, I was driving from my mother's home to my home, which was a good one-hour drive. I was getting on the freeway. It was dark and raining, and I could not see where I was going. I was following the ramp around on the left and didn't realize I was depending on the concrete wall for guidance until it stopped. Quite by accident, I went straight across and found myself going into the other lane of traffic. There was a pool of water in front of me. I felt I shouldn't get any closer to the water because I thought it could possibly be deep. I did get turned around and went the long way home and arrived safely. Several days later, I went back to where this incident happened. I realized I could have torn up my car as well as gotten into the deep pool of water and possibly drowned. I felt angels helped me and protected me from a possible tragedy.

I'm sure all of us can reflect back on a time when we felt there must have been an angel present. If we feel the need of an angel, we need to pray for God to send one or many. But sometimes circumstances are such that we don't have time to ask for one or see the need for one until it is too late. That is why it is comforting to know that God is watching over us and sends angels our way whether we ask for one or not.

ANGELS

Beautiful angels sent from above
To protect us through His omnipotent love
With comfort, love, mercy and grace
Fresh every morning to set the pace

12

GOD IN ALL HIS GLORY

Many times, as individuals, we feel that God does not love us or that we are unworthy of His love for many different reasons. We feel that we are not smart enough or that we are not pretty or handsome enough for God to love us. We feel He does not love us because we live on the wrong side of the tracks or that we have lived too sinful a life. We feel He does not love us because we have made too many mistakes or that He doesn't know we exist. Whatever the reason we feel God does not care about us, it is far from the truth and is another one of Satan's lies.

God loves each and every one of us and accepts us no matter what our condition or status in life. If we have accepted God into our lives, God has called us His friends. And He is a Friend that will stay closer than a brother. (Proverbs 18:24)

If we have accepted Christ as our Savior, we are born of God and the evil one cannot touch us, meaning he cannot touch our spirit. (I John 5:18) This is not to say that Satan is not in this world or that he will not try to hinder us in what we are doing or try to influence our decisions. Satan is here in this world to kill, steal and destroy our lives, if we allow it. (John 10:10) He is here to do everything in his power to make us miserable and to keep us from succeeding in doing God's will for our life. God considers us His Saints. (Ephesians 1:1) We are saved by the grace of God. Salvation is for the Glory of God and for us to see the greatness of His power. God also considers us His children (John 1:12), and we have direct access to God through the Holy Spirit. (Ephesians 2:18) God is our faithful Creator, and through His word, we can see His miracles and His power. When we are saved, God sends down the Holy Spirit to dwell within each one of us to help us and to guide us.

We have been adopted into God's family (Ephesians 1:5), and we are a member of Christ's body. (I Corinthians 12:27) We are united with the Lord, and we are one Spirit with Him. (I Corinthians 6:17) As Christians, we are all members of the body of Christ. We may feel we don't care for another member of the body, or we may feel we don't need another member. But in truth, we all need each other. Just as a physical body needs all the limbs and parts of its body to function, we are the same. We need each other, and we are to minister and care for each other as one body. When we are a part of God's family:

"Therefore, having been justified by faith, we have peace with God through our Lord Jesus Christ, through whom we also have access by faith into this grace in which we stand, and rejoice in hope of the glory of God." Romans 5:1-2

We have been bought with a price (I Corinthians 6:20), and we have been redeemed and forgiven of all our sins. (Colossians 1:14) We have been bought, through the blood of our Lord and Savior, Jesus Christ. We, as believers, are to be used by God and we are to glorify His name.

We should remember we are free from all condemnation (Romans 8:1-2) because God sent His Son to die in our place so that we could have eternal life with Him. We cannot be separated from the love of God, (Romans 8:35) because we are established, anointed and sealed by God. (II Corinthians 1:20-22) We are hidden with Christ in God. (Colossians 3:3) The Father, Son and Spirit of God are for us, and" If God is for us who can be against us?" Romans 8:31

"And we know that all things work together for good to those who love the Lord, to those who are called according to His purpose." Romans 8:28

All of the circumstances of life work out for our good, even though at times it may be extremely painful for us to endure some of the things we have to go through.

To God's children, God's throne is a throne of grace and mercy. If we are tempted or have troubles, we can come to God for help. If we have sinned, we may come to Him for forgiveness in our time of need.

If we have a spirit of fear in anything we are doing, this comes from Satan. We need to ask God to take away our fear because He has already given to us His power, His love and His mind to do all that we need to accomplish. "There is no fear in love; but perfect love cast out fear, because fear involves torment. But he who fears has not been made perfect in love." I John 4:18

We are the salt and light of the world. (Matthew 5:13-14) We, as Christians, are to be the salt, for salt arrests the decay in the world. We are to allow the light of God to shine through us to unbelievers, hoping to win them to Christ.

We are Christ's personal witness (Acts 1:8), and God's co-worker. (II Corinthians 6:1) God's power is available to us as His witnesses. We should want to work with God by witnessing to others and doing for them and thinking of them more highly than ourselves.

Our body is the Temple of God (I Corinthians 3:16); therefore, we should act accordingly and eat or drink in moderation. We should refuse to harm our bodies with drugs, alcohol or anything that could destroy them. God said,

"You did not choose Me, but I chose you and appointed you that you should go and bear fruit, and that your fruit should remain, that whatever you ask the Father in My name He may give you." John 15:16

God chose us for the purpose of serving Him. God has a plan for each of our lives, and we are to work according to His plan. We are all made different and have a different plan; therefore, we should not compare ourselves to each other. We all have our strengths and weaknesses. He chose us to become what He wants us to be, and that is to be more like Him.

We are a branch of the True Vine, a channel of His life. (John 15:1-5) God is the True Vine, and we are the branches. A branch is to produce good fruit. God sees where we are lacking in some way and prunes us to produce good fruit so we may have godly, productive lives. We are God's workmanship (Ephesians 2:10), and we are significant to God. God created each one of us so we could have life and have it to the fullest. He created us for His enjoyment, and we are of value to Him.

Our God is Love to the loveless; He is Peace to the restless; He is Hope to the hopeless; and He is Light to the darkness. He is our Strength and our Joy.

We are seated with Christ in the heavenly realm. (Ephesians 2:6) Lost people are in bondage to the world. Christ came so that we may be set free from all bondage. Through our union with Christ by faith, we will have blessings here on earth and eternal blessings with Christ in Heaven, for we are eternal citizens in Heaven. (Philippians 3:20)

We may approach the throne of grace with freedom and confidence (Ephesians 3:12) through prayer, knowing anytime we have a need or just want to talk to God, He is there to listen and answer. With God's help, the good work that God has begun in us will be perfected. (Philippians 1:6)

With God's help, we can do whatever God has called us to do. He never gives us anything to do that He cannot do through us. He will equip, guide and direct us. With all of these things in mind, we should have the confidence to do anything Christ would have us do.

Now that we know who we are in Christ, let's find out who Christ is and the benefits of praising Him.

Christ is the King of Kings. (I Timothy 6:15)

He is the God of Gods. (Hebrews 1:8)

He is the Lord of Lords. (Deuteronomy 10:17)

He is the Lord who made all things. (Isaiah 44:24)

He is the Creator. (John 1:3)

He is the Christ. (I John 2:2)

He is the Author of Life. (Acts 3:15)

He is the Word of God. (John 1:1)

He is the Deliverer. (Romans 11:26)

He is the Ruler of God's creation. (Revelation 3:14)

He is our Advocate. (I John 2:1)

He is Alpha and Omega. The beginning and the end.(Revelation 1:8; 22:13)

He is the First and the Last. (Revelation 1:17)

He is the Firstborn from the dead. (Revelation 1:5)

He is the Almighty. (Revelation 1:8)

He is the I Am. (John 8:58)

He is the God of the King of Heaven. (Daniel 4:37)

He is the King of the Jews. (Matthew 2:2)

He is the King of Israel. (John 1:49)

He is the King of all the Ages. (I Timothy 1:17)

He is the King of Glory. (Psalm 24:7)

He is the King of the Saints. (Revelation 15:3)
He is the Prince of the King of the Earth.
    (Revelation 1:5)
He is King Eternal. (I Timothy 1:17)
He is Immanuel. (Matthew 1:23)
He is the Lion of the Tribe of Judah.
    (Revelation 5:5)
He is our Wonderful Counselor. (Isaiah 9:6)
He is the Horn of Salvation. (Luke 1:69)
He is the Image of God. (II Corinthians 4:4)
He is our Cornerstone. (I Peter 2:6)
He is Lord of all. (Acts 10:36)
He is the Mediator of the New Covenant.
    (Hebrews 9:15)
He is the Stone the builders rejected. (Acts 4:11)
He is our Sacrificed Passover Lamb.
    (I Corinthians 5:7)
He is the Faithful and True Witness.
    (Revelation 3:14)
He is the Righteous One. (Acts 7:52)
He is the Resurrection and Life. (John 11:25)
He is our Redemption. (I Corinthians 1:30)
He is the Son of God. (John 1:49)
He is Truth. (John 14:6)
He is Life. (John 14:6)
He is the Atoning Sacrifice of our Sins. (I John 2:2)
He is the Judge to the living and the dead.
    (Acts 10:42)
He is the Husband to the widows. (Psalm 146:9))
He is Holiness. (I Corinthians 1:30)
He is our Hope. (Timothy 1:1)
He is our Hope of Glory. (Colossians1:23)

He is the Perfecter of our Faith. (Hebrews 12:2)

He is our Mighty Fortress. (I Corinthians 10:4)

He is the Good Shepherd. (Hebrews 13:20)

He is the Living Stone. (I Peter 2:4)

He is the Light of the World. (John 8:12)

He is Holiness. (I Corinthians 1:30)

He is the Power of God. (I Corinthians 1:24)

He is our Rabbi. (Matthew 26:25)

He is our Hope of Glory. (Colossians 1:27)

He is our Prophet. (Acts 3:22)

He is the One True Vine. (John 15:1)

He is the Truth and the Way. (John 14:6)

He is Faithful and True. (Revelation 19:11)

He is the Word of God. (Revelation 19:13)

He is the Wisdom of God. (I Corinthians 1:24)

He is the Righteous One. (Acts 7:52)

He is the Son of the Most High God. (Luke 1:32)

He is the Son of David. (Luke 18:39)

He is the Begotten Son of God. (John 1:18)

He is the Morning Star. (Revelation 22:16)

He is the Source of Eternal Salvation for all who
obey Him. (Hebrews 5:9)

He is the Great High Priest. (Hebrews 4:14)

He is the Lamb of God. (John 1:29)

He is the Lamb without Blemish. (I Peter 1:19)

He is the Bread of God. (John 6:33)

He is the Atoning Sacrifice for our Sins. (I John 2:2)

He is the Bridegroom. (Matthew 9:15)

He is the Head of the Church. (Ephesians 1:22)

He is Eternal Life. (I John 1:2)

He is our Amen, Faithful and True Witness.
(Revelation 3:14)
He is all we need!

Glory and all praise are to God! When we worship and praise God, it enhances our appreciation of Him, and our love grows for Him. When we worship and praise God, it expands our vision and energizes our work. Our spirit is refreshed, and it calms our fears when we worship and praise God's name. Satan should tremble when the saints pray because the angels are working on our behalf and God is answering our prayers. Our worship and praise prepare us for Heaven, and give us something to look forward to. We need to do the work and run the race God has set before us. (I Corinthians 9:24)

It is God's goal for each of His Saints to become Christ-like, more like His Son. (Hebrews 12:14) God wants us to be sanctified through the truth of God's word. Every truth that we learn leads us closer to holiness.

God never told us that our journey here on earth would be an easy one. As we go along life's journey, sometimes it is painful. We encounter many trials and tribulations. We are to learn through our trials to be like Jesus. If we don't learn the first time, we have to repeat some of the same trials again until we learn what God would have us to learn. God works through our pain and trials to bring Glory to Himself and to help us learn more about Him. Jesus suffered so that through His sufferings, we could see His Glory and could see the way to truth and true joy. There is no greater joy on earth than to be in the center of God's will and to receive God's greatest blessings. This life on earth is a dress-rehearsal for the things to come. To have real joy, we should live whole-heartedly for Christ and selflessly for others. We should pray for joy daily so as to gain strength from the Lord. They go hand in hand.

"The joy of the Lord is your strength." Nehemiah 8:10

Nehemiah was a Jewish man in captivity and the king's cupbearer, a layman who loved Jerusalem. When he had heard about the poor and aged condition of the walls and gates of the city of Jerusalem, he asked the king if he could go and rebuild them. He was concerned about the welfare of the Jewish people in Jerusalem. The people were no longer powerful, and the city of Jerusalem was in ruins.

Nehemiah was a man of prayer and still believed in a great God. Through much prayer, Nehemiah made himself available to God and was allowed to go see for himself what needed to be done.

In God's timing, Nehemiah enlisted the best leaders and became personally acquainted with the needs of the people. At the right time, Nehemiah and the workers began to repair and rebuild the walls and the gates to the city.

Anytime God's people are doing the work given by God, there will be opposition. Nehemiah had his share. The enemy (Satan) was attacking from inside the nation with selfishness and greed among the people. The enemy was attacking with accusations of slander against Nehemiah and fear from "family informers," opposing the work. But Nehemiah and the Jewish people chose through determination and faith to continue to rebuild and fortify the city's walls and gates and not listen to these threats and accusations.

Nehemiah practiced great leadership and was a true shepherd of God. Through fervent prayer and thorough preparation, the walls and gates were rebuilt, in spite of the opposition.

Before the rebuilding of the walls and gates, Ezra, a prophet, was already in Jerusalem restoring the laws of the Israelite people. When the walls and gates were completed, Ezra held a huge "Bible Conference" during the Feast of Tabernacles. The Israelites honored God's word by standing and listening to the word when it was read and by seeking to understand the word. They were there to praise God's name and rejoice in hearing the word of God.

It is one thing to hear the word of God, but it is something quite different to obey the word of God. When we are in right standing with God, we want to obey His word and support His work.

How do the heart and obedience of Nehemiah and Israel apply to our lives today? It is no different for us than it was for them. We must not get ahead of the Lord but do the work according to God's plans. God sees the whole picture, whereas we are inclined to have tunnel vision. All we see at times is what pertains to us. Nehemiah was not working to make things better for himself. He was working to restore a nation that was broken down and devastated. That is why prayer is so important when we are trying to do God's will.

Prayer allows us to leave the situation in God's hands and will help us to see the situation clearly through God's eyes, not ours. Prayer will help us to quiet our heart as we wait on the Lord to work. God's word says:

" Be anxious for nothing, but in everything by prayer and supplication, with thanksgiving, let your request be known to God." Philippians 4:6

Prayer also activates our faith and helps us to focus on God and not on ourselves. It helps to build our trust. God can accomplish the things that we cannot. When problems come our way, we should immediately take them to God and leave them and allow Him to work out the situation.

"We also glory in tribulations, knowing that tribulation produces perseverance; and perseverance character; and character, hope. Now hope does not disappoint, because the love of God has been poured out in our hearts by the Holy Spirit who was given to us." Romans 5:3-5

Any work that is done on God's behalf only succeeds because of God working through us. If we take the credit, God is not glorified, and we become proud and puffed up. The work becomes an idol, taking God's place.

May we sing God's praises daily, even when we can't see Him working in our lives. May we rejoice in knowing that His Presence is real, feeling His tenderness toward His people. May we take the time to seek Him each and every day, knowing that He loves us and will never forsake us.

Praise is to the God of Gods and Lord of Lords! Amen! And Amen!

RESOURCES

Meyer, Joyce. *The Everyday Life Bible*, amplified version. Zondervan Corporation, Hachette Book Group USA 1271 Avenue of the Americas, New York, NY 10020, 1987

The Holy Bible, New King James Version. Thomas Nelson Publisher, Box 141000, Nashville, Tennessee 37214-1000, 1982

Knoll, Woodrow. *When God Doesn't Answer*. Baker Book House Co. Grand Rapids, Michigan, 49516-6287, 1997

Epp, Theodore. Moses VI *God Prepares His Man*. Back to the Bible Broadcast, Box 82808 Lincoln, Nebraska 68501, 1975

Epp, Theodore. Moses VII *God Strengthens His Man*. Back to the Bible Broadcast, Box 82808 Lincoln, Nebraska 6850, 1975

Epp, Theodore. Moses VIII *Great Leader and Lawgiver*. Back to the Bible Broadcast, Box 82808, Lincoln, Nebraska 6850, 1976

Epp, Theodore. Moses VIV *Moses Greatest Moments*. Back to the Bible Broadcast, Box 82808 Lincoln, Nebraska 68501, 1976

Heflin, Ward Ruth. *Glory* McDougal Publishing, Hagers Town, Maryland, 1999

Van Gorder, Paul R. *The Old Testament Presents Reflections of Christ* Radio Bible Class Grand Rapids, Michigan, 1982

Epp, Theodore. *Portraits of Christ in the Tabernacle* Back to the Bible Broadcast Lincoln, Nebraska 68501, 1976

Levy, David M. *The Tabernacle, Shadows of the Messiah*, the Friends of Israel Gospel Ministry, Box 908, Bellmawr, New Jersey 08099, 1993

Perry, J.H. *The Book of Jasher*, Artisan Publishers, Box 1529, Muskogee, Oklahoma 74402 Copyright 1988Box 635, Lynnwood, Washington 98046, 1995

Bounds, E.M. *Obtaining Answers to Prayers*, Whitaker House, Pittsburg and Colflax St. Springdale, Pennsylvania 15144, 1984

Jeremiah, David. *Prayer, the Great Adventure,* Multnomah Publishers Inc., Sister, Oregon, 1997

Hamblin, William J. & Rolph, David Seely., *Solomon's Temple* Library Myth and History, Thames and Hudson Inc., 500 Fifth Ave. New, York, N.Y. 10110, 2007

Goldhill, Simon. *The Temple of Jerusalem,* Profile Books Ltd. 58A Hatton Garden, London, Ecin 8LX, 2004

Davis, John J. & Whitcomb, John C., *Israel,* Baker Book House, Grand Rapids, Michigan 49506, 1989

Ederskeim, Alfred. *The Temple: its Ministry and Services,* Erdman's Publishing Co., Grand Rapids, Michigan, 1975

Scott, Bruce. *The Feast of Israel, Seasons of the Messiah,* the Friends of Israel Gospel Ministry, Inc., Bellmawr, New Jersey 08099, 1997

Olitzky, Rabbi Kerry M. & Judson, Rabbi Daniel. *Jewish Holidays, a Brief Introduction for Christians.* Jewish Lights Publishing, Woodstock, Vermont, 2007

Glaze, Bob. *A Historical and Prophetic Study of Angels,* Hearthstone Publishing LTD 500 Beacon Dr., Oklahoma City, Oklahoma 73127, 1998

Hutchins N.W. & Glaze Bob. *Angels from Genesis to Revelation* Hearthstone Publishing, 500 Beacon Dr. Oklahoma City, Oklahoma 73127, 1997

Showers, Ronald. *Those Invisible Spirits Called Angels*, Friends of Israel Gospel Ministry, Bellmawr, New jersey 08099, 1997

Oxford American Dictionary, Oxford University Press, Inc., 198 Madison Ave., New York, N.Y. 10016, 2006

ENDNOTES

Chapter 1

Everyday Life Bible, By Joyce Meyer, amplified version. Zondervan Corporation Hachett Group USA, 1271 Avenue of the America's, New York, N.Y. 10020 P. 17

Chapter 5

Glory, By Ruth Ward Heflin, Glory McDougal Publishing, Hagers Town, Maryland 1999 P. 47

About the Author

Pamela Sweeden is a native of Arkansas, residing in Little Rock. She has been a cosmetologist for thirty-five years and owned her own business for twenty years. She was a prayer coordinator for a local church for six years and spoke in various churches and retirement homes about prayer during this time. She is currently a member of Temple Baptist Church in Little Rock. Pamela's desire is for each person to have a fervent heart for prayer and to be transformed into the likeness of Christ through prayer.

Breinigsville, PA USA
17 February 2010
232628BV00001B/2/P